Lanzarote
Travel Guide 2024

Hike Volcanoes, Dine in Caves, Unwind in Paradise

Adam O. Frady

Copyright © **Adam O. Frady**, 2024.

All rights reserved. No part of this publication may be reproduced, distributed, or transmitted in any form or by any means, including photocopying, recording, or other electronic or mechanical methods, without the prior written permission of the publisher, except in the case of brief quotations embodied in critical reviews and certain other non-commercial uses permitted by copyright law.

CONTENTS

My Lanzarote Trip

Introduction

Overview

What Makes Lanzarote Unique

Getting to Know Lanzarote

Geography and Climate

History and Culture

Flora and Fauna

Planning Your Trip

Best Time to Visit

How to Get to Lanzarote

Visa Requirements and Travel Documents

Budgeting for Your Trip

Regions and Towns

Exploring Arrecife: The Capital City

Discovering Playa Blanca

Venturing into Puerto del Carmen

Roaming Around Teguise

Exploring Other Notable Towns and Villages

Top Attractions

Timanfaya National Park

Jameos del Agua: Unique Underground Caves

César Manrique Foundation

Famara Beach: Surfing Paradise

Mirador del Río: Spectacular Viewpoint

Cactus Garden: Botanical Wonder

El Golfo: Green Lagoon and Black Sand Beach

Outdoor Activities

Hiking and Trekking Trails

Cycling Routes

Watersports

Diving and Snorkeling Spots

Camel Rides and Jeep Safaris

Cultural Experiences

Museums and Art Galleries

Historical Sites and Archaeological Sites

Canarian Cuisine and Gastronomy

Traditional Festivals and Events

Local Markets and Crafts

Practical Information

Accommodation Options
- Hotels
- Resorts
- Villas
- Apartments

Dining and Eating Out

Transportation

Safety Tips and Emergency Contacts

Insider's Guide

Off the Beaten Path Attractions

Hidden Gems and Secret Spots

Tips for Immersing Yourself

Itinerary

7 Days Itinerary

My Lanzarote Trip

Lanzarote was unlike any place I'd ever encountered before. From the moment I stepped off the plane, the stark beauty of the island seized me. The arid landscape, a tapestry of volcanic reds, browns, and blacks, sprawled beneath an impossibly blue sky. It felt like I'd stepped onto another planet, one where the scars of ancient eruptions were etched into the very earth.

The air carried a warmth I hadn't expected, a gentle heat infused with the tang of salt and the faintest hint of sulfur. As I made my way to the quaint, whitewashed village where I would stay, the landscape morphed. Cacti sprouted like alien guardians from the unforgiving soil, their silhouettes stark against the rolling hills. Fields of grapes, somehow thriving in this unique environment, created patches of vibrant green. It was a testament to the resilience of nature and the islanders who worked in harmony with it.

My days unfolded in a leisurely rhythm. Mornings were spent exploring the beaches. Some were wide swaths of golden sand, lapped by turquoise waters, while others were hidden coves, their black volcanic sands creating a stark and mesmerizing beauty. The Atlantic wind, ever-present, whipped my hair into a frenzy and cooled my skin. Yet, beneath the surface, the ocean was surprisingly comfortable, and I spent hours discovering rock pools teeming with life and snorkeling off pristine shores.

One afternoon, I ventured into Timanfaya National Park – the heart of the island's volcanic fire. The landscape transformed into a desolate, lunar-like expanse. Craters dotted the earth like giant pockmarks, and jagged lava flows stretched endlessly toward the horizon. As I hiked into this surreal terrain, I could feel the silent power of the slumbering volcanoes beneath my feet.

Later on that same trip, I descended into Cueva de los Verdes, a labyrinth of underground lava tubes. The cavernous world felt ancient, the air moist against my skin. Eerie illumination highlighted fantastical rock formations, showcasing the raw power of molten earth frozen in time.

Back in the sunshine, I found myself drawn to the legacy of César Manrique, an artist whose vision shaped Lanzarote. His creations were a harmonious blend of art and nature. Jameos del Agua, built into a volcanic crater, showcased a stunning saltwater lagoon teeming with life, while his former home, Taro de Tahíche, melted seamlessly into a lava field, a bold architectural statement in stark contrast to its natural surroundings.

Evenings melted into a kaleidoscope of vibrant sunsets, painting the sky in streaks of orange, purple, and crimson. I'd savor long meals in local restaurants, the flavors of the island dancing on my tongue. Fresh seafood, simply prepared, tasted of the ocean it came from. Wrinkled potatoes, grown in nutrient-rich volcanic soil, were accompanied by fiery mojo sauces. Local wines, carrying the faintest echo of minerals, became my companions as I watched the stars paint the night sky.

As my trip came to a close, I felt a profound sense of change wash over me. Lanzarote was a place of raw beauty and surprising contrasts. Its harsh landscape had ignited a deep appreciation for the tenacity of life. Its unique blend of nature and art sparked my imagination. I left Lanzarote carrying more than memories or souvenirs; I carried a sense of wonder, inspired by an island that had shown me a whole new definition of beauty.

Introduction

Overview

Lanzarote, a Spanish island nestled within the captivating Canary Islands, is a place where dramatic volcanic landscapes, warm weather, and unique artistic touches intertwine. Located in the Atlantic Ocean, Lanzarote holds the distinction of being the easternmost island in the archipelago. It lies approximately 125 kilometers off the North African coast and about 1,000 kilometers away from the Iberian Peninsula.

Lanzarote's story began about 15 million years ago when volcanic forces sculpted it from the depths of the earth. Evidence of its fiery origin is everywhere – over 300 volcanic cones dot the landscape, lava fields stretch across the terrain, and striking black sand beaches hug the coastline. This otherworldly environment offers extraordinary sights like Timanfaya National Park, a testament to the island's powerful geological past. Here, visitors witness a dormant volcanic landscape where the earth still simmers just below the surface.

Beyond Timanfaya, Lanzarote invites exploration of other natural wonders. The Cueva de los Verdes is a remarkable lava tube system, a subterranean marvel formed by ancient eruptions. Mirador del Rio, a stunning viewpoint, offers breathtaking panoramas of the island and its neighboring islets.

A Climate of Sunshine and Gentle Rains

Lanzarote enjoys a dry and mild climate, a perfect complement to its volcanic terrain. The sun shines brightly, with average annual temperatures hovering around a delightful 21.9°C, balanced by gentle rainfall averaging just 144 mm per year. This consistent weather pattern makes it an ideal escape for sun-seekers almost any time of year.

The Legacy of César Manrique

The island is not only a natural marvel but also bears the remarkable artistic vision of local artist and architect César Manrique. A true visionary, Manrique championed a beautiful balance between Lanzarote's natural wonders and human creations. His works are woven into the island's fabric: the enchanting Jardin de Cactus, a botanical garden showcasing cacti from around the world; the Fundación César Manrique, his former home transformed into an artistic space; and the Jameos del Agua, a series of lava caves artfully integrated into a cultural and leisure complex.

A UNESCO Biosphere Reserve and Biodiversity Hotspot

Lanzarote's remarkable environmental value earned it the distinguished title of Biosphere Reserve from UNESCO in 1993. This recognition highlights the island's diverse ecosystems that support a wealth of plant, animal, and marine life – a testament to the ecological importance of this unique Atlantic gem.

With over 3 million visitors each year, Lanzarote has emerged as a beloved tourist destination for good reason. Adventures await in a variety of forms: camel rides across the volcanic landscapes, endless opportunities for water sports, scenic hikes, cycling tours, golf, and even exploring the local winemaking traditions through tasting experiences. The island has built a solid infrastructure to support tourism, including an international airport, seaport, and reliable transportation system.

Arrecife and Beyond

Arrecife, Lanzarote's capital and largest city, is its beating commercial and administrative heart. However, the island's charms extend to other towns, each with its own distinct flavor: Puerto del Carmen, a bustling tourist resort; Playa Blanca, offering a more relaxed resort experience; Costa Teguise, popular for watersports; and Haría, a tranquil village nestled in the beautiful Valley of a Thousand Palms.

What Makes Lanzarote Unique

Lanzarote, a Spanish jewel in the Atlantic, stands apart from its neighbors in the Canary Islands for reasons both dramatic and subtle. It is an island where earth, fire, and human creativity have converged to shape a landscape and culture unlike any other.

The legacy of Lanzarote's birth is etched upon every inch of its terrain. This is a volcanic land, a place where the very ground beneath your feet tells tales of molten rock and fiery eruptions. Over 300 volcanic cones rise like ancient sentinels across the island, their presence a constant reminder of the powerful forces that sculpted this place. Lava fields, stark and captivating, spread across the land, and beaches of impossibly black sand speak of the ocean's dance with the fiery heart of the Earth.

The island's volcanic origins are more than a visual spectacle; they hold historical echoes as well. Lanzarote's recent volcanic eruptions, as late as the 18th and 19th centuries, have created a lunar-like landscape so otherworldly that NASA once used it to test its moon buggies. The Montañas del Fuego, the Fire Mountains, showcase nearly 100 volcanoes, painting an almost Martian scene across Lanzarote's interior. This dramatic quarter of the island is protected within Timanfaya National Park, a testament to the raw, untamed beauty of volcanic power.

Where Art and Nature Intertwine

But Lanzarote is not only a product of natural forces. It bears the indelible mark of human artistry, a legacy spearheaded by the revered César Manrique. This son of Lanzarote was a visionary artist and architect, a man who saw not conflict, but harmony, between the island's rugged beauty and the touch of the human hand. Manrique's profound influence permeates the island's built environment; structures blend seamlessly into the landscape, echoing the volcanic forms through the use of natural stone and traditional styling.

Manrique's own creations are must-see attractions themselves: the Jardin de Cactus, a botanical wonderland showcasing cacti from across the globe; the Fundación César Manrique, where his former home is now a captivating art space; and perhaps most mesmerizing of all, the Jameos del Agua. Here, Manrique transformed a series of lava caves into a stunning complex, a fusion of nature's raw form and his avant-garde artistic vision.

An Island of Flavors, Culture, and Conservation

Lanzarote's uniqueness extends to its culinary traditions, a delightful blend of Spanish and African influences. Fresh seafood, island-grown vegetables, and a touch of spice come together to create flavors that reflect the island's vibrant spirit. Nights on Lanzarote offer their own magic with a range of bars, clubs, and restaurants catering to varied tastes and energy levels.

Lanzarote's commitment to conservation earned it the designation of a UNESCO Biosphere Reserve in 1993. Unique flora and fauna, including rare endemic species like the Canarian palm and the Lanzarote shrew, thrive alongside a dazzling array of marine life. Dolphins, whales, and sea turtles are all visitors to Lanzarote's waters. The island actively promotes ecotourism and the protection of its natural treasures. Hiking and cycling trails wind through the landscape, offering opportunities for quiet exploration.

Getting to Know Lanzarote

Geography and Climate

A Spanish archipelago nestled in the vast Atlantic Ocean, the Canary Islands themselves are a product of volcanic activity; Lanzarote, as the easternmost and fourth-largest of the group, holds a special place in this geological legacy.

The island's story begins some 15 million years ago when it emerged from the depths as molten rock spewed forth from the Canary hotspot – a mantle plume churning beneath the Earth's crust, responsible for the archipelago's existence. Today, the evidence of Lanzarote's birth is everywhere. Over 300 volcanic cones pierce the landscape, some still slumbering, others holding the memory of their fiery past in the stark and beautiful landscapes they have left behind.

The most dramatic reminder of Lanzarote's volcanic heritage is Timanfaya National Park. Here, nearly 100 volcanoes stretch across the terrain, their presence so evocative of the Martian landscape that scientists once chose this spot to test lunar exploration vehicles. This protected area showcases the raw power of volcanic eruptions, particularly those of the 18th and 19th centuries that forever reshaped the island's heart.

Volcanoes, Cacti, and Hidden Caves

The visual tapestry of Lanzarote is a striking mix of rugged textures and surprising beauty. Lava fields snake across the land, frozen reminders of fiery rivers that once flowed, while beaches of impossibly black sand speak of the ocean's dance with the island's volcanic heart. But Lanzarote also boasts natural wonders of a different sort. The Cueva de los Verdes is a testament to the molten rock's artistry, a lava tube sculpted into a breathtaking natural tunnel. Another volcanic creation, the Jameos del Agua, showcases a series of caves harboring a saltwater lake and a remarkable species – tiny blind albino crabs found nowhere else on Earth.

For those seeking stunning vistas, the Mirador del Rio perches high above the island, offering sweeping panoramas of Lanzarote itself and the neighboring islet of La Graciosa. Plant lovers will find themselves drawn to the Jardin de Cactus, a botanical marvel showcasing over 10,000 cacti gathered from the far corners of the globe.

The Winds, the Sun, and the Unique Climate

Lanzarote enjoys an arid climate shaped by its unique position and the steady presence of trade winds. These breezes blow consistently from the northeast, particularly in the afternoons, bringing relief from the warm temperatures which average a comfortable 21.9°C (71.4°F) throughout the year. Occasionally, the winds shift, and the 'calima' arrives – a hot blast from the African continent that carries dust or sand from the desert, reducing visibility and raising temperatures significantly for a short time.

Although Lanzarote experiences four seasons, the transitions are subtle. Winters are mild and sunny, a haven for those seeking respite from harsher climates. Spring arrives with warmth and dryness, while summers are predictably hot with clear skies and endless sunshine.

Autumn brings a touch more humidity but remains warm and inviting.

A Haven for Travelers and Adventurers
The island's unique geography and pleasant climate create an ideal environment for travelers seeking something beyond the usual beach holiday. Camel rides through the volcanic landscape offer a unique twist on exploration, while the diverse coastline invites a plethora of watersports. Hikers and cyclists can lose themselves on trails winding through otherworldly terrain, while those seeking a more relaxed pace can enjoy a round of golf amidst the volcanic scenery. Foodies will delight in Lanzarote's winemaking tradition and the fresh flavors of its gastronomy.

For all its natural wonders, visitors will find Lanzarote well-equipped with the infrastructure necessary for comfortable tourism. An international airport and seaport connect it to the world, while a reliable network of roads and public transport makes exploring the island a breeze. Arrecife, the capital and largest city, is the island's bustling commercial hub. However, those seeking a taste of Lanzarote's charm will find it in the smaller towns like Puerto del Carmen, Playa Blanca, Costa Teguise, and the tranquil village of Haría.

History and Culture

Lanzarote's history unfolds like an epic poem, marked by volcanic beginnings, the arrival of new peoples, and a struggle to thrive amidst both natural hardship and the ambitions of empires. The island's story begins far back in time, approximately 15 million years ago, when fiery eruptions wrenched it from the ocean's depths. This places it among the oldest of the Canary Islands, a chain forged by the same volcanic forces.

Long before European eyes fell upon Lanzarote, it was known as Tyterogaka by the Majos, a people of Berber origin believed to have arrived around 1000 BC. They lived lives steeped in tradition, centered around animal husbandry and a simple, pastoral existence. But the Majos' world was forever altered in the 14th century when

European explorers began to chart the Atlantic. It was Lancelotto Malocello, a navigator from Genoa, who bestowed the island's contemporary name.

The year 1402 was a turning point, as the French nobleman Jean de Bethencourt, backed by the Castilian crown, successfully conquered the island. Lanzarote was transformed again when a Castilian noble, Diego de Herrera, was granted rule, establishing a feudal lordship that endured until 1812. This was a turbulent era, the peace of island life frequently shattered by invaders seeking plunder and slaves. Pirates from France, Morocco, and Britain all took their turns at exploiting the island's resources and people.

Mother Nature herself also dealt harsh blows. The devastating volcanic eruptions between 1730 and 1736 laid waste to a quarter of Lanzarote, forcing a wave of emigration from the now ash-covered landscape. Despite these setbacks, the island demonstrated a remarkable resilience. Agriculture gradually recovered, commerce bloomed, and vital infrastructure slowly took shape.

Further economic growth came in 1852 when Lanzarote was designated a free-trade zone. By 1927, the island was fully integrated into the province of Las Palmas. This march of progress led to 1982, a monumental year when the Canary Islands, Lanzarote included, gained autonomy. And in 1993, global recognition of Lanzarote's ecological significance came in the form of a UNESCO Biosphere Reserve designation.

Culture: Art, Tradition, and Island Flavors

Lanzarote's culture is a vibrant tapestry woven from Spanish and African influences, interlaced with a deep respect for the environment and an artistic spirit that permeates daily life. César Manrique stands as the undisputed champion of this unique cultural identity. Born and raised on Lanzarote, this visionary artist and architect dedicated his life to ensuring that structures built on the island would coexist harmoniously with the natural landscape. Traditional materials like wood and stone took center stage in his designs, always with an eye towards respecting the land's stark beauty.

Manrique left his creative mark on many of Lanzarote's most beloved landmarks. The Jardin de Cactus bursts with botanical life; the Fundación César Manrique – his former home transformed into an artistic haven – celebrates his life and work; and the Jameos del Agua showcases his playful incorporation of volcanic features into a mesmerizing cultural complex. Beyond these creations, Manrique fiercely advocated for responsible, sustainable development that would protect his beloved island from the ravages of mass tourism and unchecked urbanization.

The Catholic faith is deeply ingrained in Lanzarote's identity. The island's calendar is filled with religious festivals and processions, including the joyous Carnival, the solemn commemorations of Holy Week, and celebrations honoring each town's patron saint. And of course, Lanzarote's culture finds expression in its cuisine, a tantalizing mix of fresh seafood, vibrant vegetables, and a touch of spice. The confluence of African, Latin American, and mainland Spain influences is evident in dishes like 'sancocho', a satisfying fish stew, or the deceptively simple 'papas arrugadas' – wrinkled potatoes served with the legendary 'mojo' sauce. Local wine, cheese, and honey add another layer of deliciousness to the island's culinary offerings.

Music, dance, and folklore further enrich Lanzarote's cultural heart. Traditional island music evokes the past, with instruments like the 'timple' (a small guitar), drums, and flutes creating melodies handed down through generations. Dances like the 'isa', 'folia', and 'malagueña' are filled with movement and joy, keeping alive an expressive heritage. Myths and legends abound, stories of phantom riders, magical fairies, and the ever-present threat of the 'evil eye' add an air of mystery to the island's narrative. Craftsmanship shines through in Lanzarote's traditional crafts – pottery, basketry, embroidery, and jewelry all created with the pride and skill of artisans steeped in the island's artistic traditions.

Flora and Fauna

Lanzarote, with its rugged volcanic terrain and seemingly relentless sunshine, is not a place where one would expect a profusion of life. Yet, the island boasts a remarkable array of flora and fauna, with numerous species thriving in this unique environment. From the coastline to the higher elevations, Lanzarote is home to roughly 500 plant species, an impressive number considering the arid conditions. Of these, a number are found nowhere else on Earth – 16 exclusive to Lanzarote, 30 to the eastern Canary Islands, 41 to the whole Canary Island chain, and 19 found only within the Macaronesia region.

The island's vegetation zones reflect the varying conditions found from the sea to the volcanic peaks. Along the coast, salt-tolerant plants cling to life. Moving inland, the lowland zone showcases a variety of succulents, hardy shrubs, and grasses remarkable for their ability to survive on minimal rainfall. As the elevation increases in the midland zone, different species find a foothold, then give way to yet another community of plants in the island's highlands.

Some of Lanzarote's most iconic plants hold deep significance within the island's identity. The sweet tabaiba, a flowering succulent with flowing milky sap, is such a symbol of the island that it has been designated its official plant symbol. The bugloss of Lanzarote, a purple-flowered beauty, is found only on this island. Towering above the landscape in certain areas, like the lush valley of Haría, is the Canary Island palm – stately trees contributing to the largest palm grove found on the island.

But the botanical wonders don't end there. Hidden within the Jameos del Agua, a cave system formed by volcanic eruptions, lives the jameito. This tiny crab, both blind and a ghostly white, has adapted to its dark, saltwater environment and is found nowhere else in the world.

Lanzarote's animal life is influenced by a fascinating mix of factors: proximity to both Europe and Africa, the isolation of island existence, and the ever-present legacy of past volcanic activity. Approximately 40 species of vertebrates call the island home, including reptiles, mammals, and birds. Invertebrates, such as a diverse range of insects, spiders, mollusks, and crustaceans, add further complexity to the ecosystem.

The Atlantic lizard, with its speckled brown or black body, thrives here, a reminder that the Canary Islands offer a haven for these reptiles. An animal less likely to go unnoticed is the dromedary camel. Introduced centuries ago, these single-humped creatures are now synonymous with Lanzarote, offering tourists a unique way to experience the volcanic landscapes of Timanfaya National Park. Overhead, keen eyes might spot the kestrel, a common bird of prey that makes its living hunting the island's rodents, insects, and smaller birds.

Perhaps most captivating of all, the Canarian hubara is a bird whose striking appearance is matched by an elaborate courtship ritual. These large birds are adapted to the arid plains of the island and are found not only in the Canaries but also in certain regions of North Africa.

Planning Your Trip

Best Time to Visit

Lanzarote's subtropical climate means pleasant weather is a near-constant, but there are nuances to the island's temperatures, winds, and rainfall patterns throughout the year. Understanding these can help you decide the optimal time to visit based on your preferences.

The Heat of Summer

The summer months, spanning June through August, are undeniably the hottest and driest period on Lanzarote. Temperatures average a comfortable 24.5°C (76.2°F), and rain is an infrequent visitor. However, summer also brings the strongest winds. The trade winds, particularly in the afternoons, offer a welcome respite from the sunshine but can sometimes carry dust or sand from the Sahara Desert. This phenomenon, called 'calima', reduces visibility and can make temperatures spike for short periods.

The Calm of Winter

December to February mark Lanzarote's coolest months, with temperatures around 17.6°C (63.6°F). While it may see occasional rain, winter also boasts the most sunshine of the year – an average of 7 glorious hours per day.

The Sweet Spot: Spring and Autumn

For many travelers, the months falling between the extremes of summer and winter offer the most idyllic conditions. From March to May and September to November, Lanzarote enjoys mild temperatures (averaging 19.9°C /67.9°F in spring and 23.3°C /73.9°F in autumn). Rainfall remains minimal, and the island experiences calmer winds with less chance of a calima event.

Balancing Crowds and Budget

Lanzarote's popularity as a tourist destination means that visitor numbers directly impact the cost of your trip. The busiest (and most expensive) time on the island is undoubtedly the summer months of July and August, when European families flock to the island's beaches for their holidays. Other peak periods that see increased crowds and prices coincide with major European school breaks, including Easter, Christmas, and winter holidays.

For those seeking both smaller crowds and more budget-friendly prices, the low season of September to June (excluding the peak holiday periods) is ideal. Not only will you experience less crowding at major attractions, but your travel and accommodation costs will likely be noticeably lower.

The Ocean Calls

If dolphin and whale watching is high on your Lanzarote wishlist, the optimal time to visit is between April and October. This period offers the best combination of warmer water temperatures and optimal visibility, increasing your chances of unforgettable encounters. Dolphin watching excursions are available year-round, but resident species are more reliably seen, and the chance of spotting migratory species increases, during these months.

For those who love nothing more than a dip in the ocean, Lanzarote's water is both clear and inviting. The sea temperatures peak from August to October at a delightful 23°C (73.4°F) and are lowest in January through March at a still-pleasant 18°C (64.4°F). The calmer waters of the south coast tend to be slightly warmer than the more exposed northern shore. While comfortable for swimming from June to November, those sensitive to cooler temperatures may prefer a wetsuit or rashguard even in the warmer months.

The Best Time is Your Time

Ultimately, the best time to visit Lanzarote depends on your individual priorities. If your heart is set on the hottest temperatures and bustling beaches, summer may be perfect. If a quiet retreat with mild weather is what you seek, the shoulder seasons of spring and autumn will suit you best. And if budget is your primary concern, the low season may be your ideal choice. Lanzarote welcomes visitors year-round, the key is determining what factors matter most for your perfect getaway!

How to Get to Lanzarote

Lanzarote beckons travelers from near and far. Whether you begin your journey in mainland Spain, or a neighboring Canary Island, the path to Lanzarote primarily involves two modes of travel: air and sea.

Your flight will bring you to Lanzarote Airport, located just 5 kilometers from the bustling capital city of Arrecife. From the airport, you have several options for reaching your final destination on the island. Public buses provide an economical choice, taxis offer direct door-to-door service, or for the ultimate flexibility, consider renting a car and exploring the volcanic landscapes at your own pace.

From Mainland Spain: Air and Sea Options

Travelers originating in mainland Spain have the advantage of both frequent flight connections and the option of a scenic sea voyage. Major cities like Madrid, Barcelona, Valencia, Seville, and Santiago offer direct flights to Lanzarote. Your journey through the air will take roughly 3 to 4 hours, with round-trip tickets averaging around $200. Flight search engines can be invaluable in finding the best prices for your desired dates.

For those who prefer a leisurely sea journey, ferries provide an alternative way to reach Lanzarote. The port of Cádiz on Spain's southern coast serves as your departure point, with ferries operated by Trasmediterránea making the crossing to Arrecife. Expect a voyage of approximately 36 hours. Round-trip ticket prices generally hover around $300, with the option of bringing your car for an additional fee. Bear in mind that ferry service is not as frequent as flights, so advance booking is essential.

Island Hopping

If your Lanzarote adventure begins on one of its neighboring Canary Islands, fast and frequent ferry connections provide an ideal mode of transport. Companies such as Fred. Olsen Express, Naviera Armas, and Líneas Romero offer routes between Lanzarote and the islands of Fuerteventura, Gran Canaria, and Tenerife.

Travel times vary from as little as 25 minutes to a maximum of six hours, with ferry ticket prices spanning a range of roughly $35 to $160 depending on the route you choose. As with other ferry journeys, the ability to bring your car along for an additional fee adds another layer of convenience.

Should you prefer to reach Lanzarote by air from a neighboring island, direct flights are available from Fuerteventura, Gran Canaria, and Tenerife. Binter and Air Europa operate these routes that take between 30 minutes to an hour. Round-trip flight tickets generally fall between $80 to $200.

Visa Requirements and Travel Documents

Lanzarote, with its otherworldly landscapes and rich culture, draws visitors from around the globe. However, the first step in planning your trip is understanding the entry requirements based on your nationality. The good news is that for many travelers, the process is remarkably straightforward.

Citizens of the EU and Schengen Area

If you hold citizenship in any European Union (EU) or European Economic Area (EEA) nation, or a country belonging to the Schengen Agreement, your path to Lanzarote is quite simple. As Spain is a member nation in these agreements, you will not require a visa for entry. The only necessary document is either a valid passport or a national identity card. It's important to note that if you are from the UK, it's wise to check your government's travel advice website for the most up-to-date information regarding entry requirements post-Brexit.

Visa-Free Travel for Many Nations

Lanzarote, along with the rest of Spain, extends visa-free entry for stays under three months to citizens of a long list of countries. This includes nations such as Andorra, Argentina, Australia, Brazil, Canada, Chile, Colombia, Israel, Japan, Mexico, New Zealand, the United States, and many others. To enter Lanzarote, you'll simply need a valid passport.

Schengen Visas: When They're Needed

If your country of citizenship does not fall within the EU/EEA/Schengen area or on the visa-free list, you'll likely need to obtain a short-stay Schengen visa prior to your trip. This type of visa grants you entry to Lanzarote and allows travel within other Schengen countries for up to 90 days within any 180-day period. The application process requires several supporting documents, including:

- A valid passport. It must not expire within six months of your planned return date and have at least one blank page available for entry stamps.
- A fully completed and signed visa application form.
- A recent passport-style photograph of yourself.
- Proof of travel insurance. This policy must cover any potential medical expenses you may incur during your trip, including repatriation if necessary.
- Proof of accommodation. This can be confirmed hotel reservations or, if staying with friends or family, an official invitation letter from your host.
- Proof of sufficient funds. Bank statements or a letter of sponsorship can demonstrate that you have adequate

resources to support yourself during your stay in Lanzarote.

- Proof of purpose of travel. Documentation such as flight reservations, a detailed tour itinerary, or official letters from an employer or educational institution can serve this purpose.
- Visa fee. The standard fee is 80 euros for adults or 40 euros for children aged 6-12.

The Spanish embassy or consulate located in your country of residence can assist you with the Schengen visa application process. It's essential to start this process a minimum of 15 days before your planned arrival in Lanzarote. Processing times can fluctuate, so applying several weeks or even months in advance is often the wisest strategy. The embassy or consulate can also provide information on tracking the status of your visa application.

Budgeting for Your Trip

Lanzarote's stunning landscapes and welcoming atmosphere make it a highly desirable destination.

However, like most vacations, making the dream a reality requires careful budgeting. By understanding the major areas of expense and researching ahead of time, you can set realistic expectations and potentially find ways to reduce the overall cost.

Flights: The First Hurdle
The cost of your flight will naturally depend on where you begin your journey. If your adventure begins on a neighboring Canary Island, expect to pay closer to $100. It's important to remember that these are simply averages - airfare is incredibly dynamic, influenced by factors like seasonality and how far in advance you book. Utilizing a reputable flight search engine is key for finding the best deals.

Where Will You Rest Your Head?
Accommodation represents another significant portion of your travel budget. Lanzarote offers a wide array of lodging options, from hostels and guesthouses to luxury resorts. A double room in a mid-range hotel typically averages around $100 per night, but you can uncover more

budget-friendly alternatives or splurge on something truly special if you desire. As with flights, booking your accommodations in advance is a smart strategy, both for securing your ideal spot and potentially accessing better rates. Thorough research using a reliable hotel booking platform will let you compare prices and amenities, enabling you to make the choice that best balances your budget with your preferences.

The Cost of Deliciousness: Dining on Lanzarote

The good news for foodies is that dining on Lanzarote is generally quite reasonable, especially when compared to other European hotspots. Expect to pay around $15 per person for a meal at a mid-range restaurant. Of course, you can find even more economical eats at local cafes, markets, or by preparing some of your own meals if your accommodations allow. High-end dining experiences and restaurants catering to the tourist crowds in prime locations will naturally come at a premium.

Getting Around the Island

Transportation costs on Lanzarote are thankfully quite manageable. Local buses provide an affordable way to get around, with one-way fares averaging a mere $2. Taxis are more expensive but still reasonable, generally around $15 for a typical journey. For the ultimate in flexibility, consider renting a car, bicycle, or scooter. Daily rental rates tend to run between $20 to $40 depending on the type of vehicle you choose. Smart budgeting might mean utilizing a mix of options – public buses for longer journeys, taxis for the occasional splurge, and perhaps a rental car for a day or two of independent exploration.

Adventures and Attractions

The activities you choose will have a significant impact on your overall trip cost. Lanzarote boasts a wealth of attractions both natural and man-made. Entry fees for popular spots like Timanfaya National Park, the Jameos del Agua, or the Jardin de Cactus fall around $10 per person. Guided tours, watersport adventures, or dolphin-watching excursions naturally command higher prices, often in the $50 range. The budget-conscious will be happy to discover that Lanzarote also offers plenty of free or low-cost ways to have fun – hiking, cycling, swimming, or exploring local museums often won't cost you a thing.

The Daily Total and Beyond

Based on the information above, a single traveler should expect to budget approximately $176 per day for their Lanzarote trip when including accommodation, food, transportation, and activities. It's crucial to note that this is simply an average! Your actual spending will be heavily influenced by your travel style. Are you a backpacker content with simple lodgings and self-prepared meals, or do you crave the comfort and amenities of a resort? By using an online trip cost calculator and customizing it to your specific preferences, you can get a much more accurate idea of the financial resources your Lanzarote adventure will require.

Use this website to have a perfect budget for your trip: https://www.budgetyourtrip.com/spain/lanzarote

Regions and Towns

Exploring Arrecife: The Capital City

Lanzarote's capital city, Arrecife, is a place where echoes of the past intertwine with contemporary vibrancy. From humble beginnings as a small fishing village, Arrecife has blossomed into a modern city while still retaining a strong connection to its heritage. Visitors will discover a blend of historic landmarks, cultural spaces, and the inviting atmosphere of a seaside city.

Arrecife's Historic Landmarks

To understand Arrecife's story, a visit to its fortresses is a must. Castillo de San Gabriel, dating back to the 16th century, stands as a testament to the city's need to defend its shores. Built upon a tiny island linked to the city by a causeway, it now houses the fascinating International Museum of Emigration. Here, the history and culture of the Canary Islands, as well as the stories of those who emigrated from these shores, are showcased.

Another guardian of the past is Castillo de San José. This 18th-century fortress, perched atop a cliff with dramatic views of the Atlantic, was built to protect Arrecife's vital port. Today, however, it offers a different kind of treasure: the Museum of Contemporary Art. Within its walls, you'll discover works by local and international artists – including a celebration of Lanzarote's own César Manrique, an artist and architect whose influence permeates the island.

Charco de San Ginés

No visit to Arrecife is complete without experiencing the Charco de San Ginés. This natural lagoon, filled with shimmering seawater, is ringed by colorfully painted houses and fishing boats. It embodies the city's deep connection to the sea and serves as a gathering place for locals and visitors alike. Stroll the charming promenade, lined with lively bars, cafes offering delicious tapas, and shops brimming with local wares.

Churches and Culture

The Church of San Ginés, dedicated to the city's patron saint, stands as a testament to faith. This simple yet elegant 17th-century structure boasts a bell tower, a graceful dome, and a Baroque altar that speaks to the artistry of the past.

For those seeking a broader cultural experience, the Centro Insular de Cultura El Almacén offers a unique opportunity. Born of the vision of César Manrique, this cultural center occupies a converted warehouse, now transformed into a dynamic space for exhibitions, workshops, and events celebrating art and education. Even if you don't have time to see what's on display, the space itself, with Manrique's artistic touch, is worth a visit. The center also houses a cinema, library, and cafe, guaranteeing there's something to appeal to everyone.

Beaches for Every Mood

Arrecife boasts two main beaches, each catering to a slightly different vibe. Playa del Reducto, with its inviting golden sands, is the heart of the city's beachfront. Calm, clear waters make this an ideal spot for swimming and snorkeling. You won't need to wander far for amenities; a long promenade lined with swaying palm trees offers shaded benches, playgrounds, showers, toilets, and lifeguard stations. For convenient sunbathing, sunbeds are readily available for rent.

Just 2 kilometers west of the city center lies Playa del Cable. Here, you'll discover a beach of volcanic black sand and a more natural, less-developed feel. The waters tend to be a bit more active, making it a haven for surfers and kite-surfers. If seeking a tranquil spot away from the crowds, Playa del Cable delivers. While this beach is less built-up than Playa del Reducto, you'll still find practical amenities like parking, showers, and toilets.

The Adventure Calls: Watersports in Arrecife

Whether you're a seasoned watersports enthusiast or eager to dip your toe in for the first time, Arrecife provides ample opportunities. Experienced sailors will find Lanzarote Sail ready to help them embark on their seafaring journeys. This school and charter company offers courses for every skill level, along with boat rentals and exciting trips for groups of up to 12. They even organize special events such as regattas and private parties on the water.

The underwater wonders of Lanzarote beckon exploration, and Aquatis Diving Center stands ready to make your diving dreams a reality. Whether you're a novice interested in a beginner's course or a certified diver seeking thrilling excursions, their professional instructors will guide the way. Discover shipwrecks, caves, and reefs teeming with marine life. Aquatis also offers a shop, pool, and lounge area for relaxing pre or post-dive.

Big Blue Sea caters to both anglers and those who simply want to experience the thrill of being on the open ocean. Their charter trips offer the chance to try your hand at catching tuna, marlin, dorado, and other species. Snacks and drinks are provided, along with a knowledgeable guide to help you with everything from baiting your hook to identifying your catch. For those interested in marine life, Big Blue Sea dolphin-watching excursions are equipped with a hydrophone, allowing you to hear the fascinating communication of these playful creatures.

Shop Til You Drop...Then Enjoy the Nightlife

Arrecife delivers when it comes to satisfying those shopping urges and finding the perfect souvenir. Head to Calle León y Castillo, the main commercial artery pulsing through the city. Here, a vibrant mix of shops, cafes, and bars await. Browse for locally made delicacies like cheese, honey, and Lanzarote's renowned wines. Boutiques offer clothing and accessories, ensuring you can take a little bit of the island's style home with you. When it's time for a break, the many terraces provide the ideal spot to enjoy a coffee or a refreshing drink.

For a more traditional mall experience, the Deiland Shopping Center lies 3 kilometers east of the city's heart. With over 60 stores, you'll find fashion, electronics, cosmetics, and more - along with a supermarket, bowling alley, cinema, and tempting food court. Free parking and wifi make a visit to Deiland convenient and hassle-free.

As the sun sets, Arrecife's nightlife scene comes alive – particularly around the picturesque Charco de San Ginés. A myriad of bars, pubs, and clubs cater to a wide range of tastes. Establishments like La Bulla attract those who love rock, pop, and indie music, with concerts and special events adding to the fun. For those eager to dance to salsa, bachata, or reggaeton, El Agua offers a colorful atmosphere and even hosts dance classes. And if house, techno, or electronic music gets your feet moving, La Marea is the place to be, with a modern design and top-notch sound and lighting systems.

https://www.hellocanaryislands.com/lanzarote/

Explore Lanzarote Official Tourism Website to View beautiful Lanzarote Landscape/tourist destinations and other services you will need in Lanzarote.

Discovering Playa Blanca

Playa Blanca, nestled in Lanzarote's south, beckons visitors with the promise of white sand beaches, a bustling marina, and the ease of island-hopping via its convenient ferry port. Whether you're a family seeking a child-friendly escape, a couple in search of a romantic retreat, or simply someone who craves endless sunshine, Playa Blanca has something to offer.

Beaches

Playa Blanca boasts three main beaches, each with its own distinct personality – yet all within easy walking distance of the town's heart. Playa Blanca Beach is aptly named for the white sand that graces its shores. This cozy beach offers an ideal swimming spot thanks to its gentle, clear blue waters. Amenities are plentiful, including sunbeds, umbrellas, showers, toilets, and the watchful presence of a lifeguard for peace of mind. Its central location means you're never far from charming shops, cafes, and restaurants when ready for a break from the sunshine.

Heading east, you'll discover Playa Dorada Beach, also known as the "Golden Beach." Here, a generous swath of golden sand awaits, along with all the necessary amenities for a day of sunbathing and swimming. Watersports enthusiasts will appreciate the onsite center where kayaks, jet skis, and pedal boats are available for rent. Playa Dorada's proximity to Marina Rubicon makes it easy to combine beach time and a visit to this stylish marina.

Playa Flamingo, the "Pink Beach," lies to the west. Its unique pinkish sand and dazzling turquoise waters create a postcard-worthy scene. Known for its tranquility and a natural breakwater that tames the waves, this beach is particularly well-loved by families with young children. Sunbeds, umbrellas, showers, toilets, and lifeguards provide comfort and convenience. While Playa Flamingo doesn't offer the immediate proximity to the town center, hotels, bars, and restaurants are close at hand.

Marina Rubicon

Between Playa Blanca and Playa Dorada lies the Marina Rubicon, a modern haven for boat owners and landlubbers alike. With over 400 berths, this stylish marina also offers numerous ways for visitors to enjoy its charms. Stroll along the waterfront, and browse a tempting mix of boutiques, art galleries, and shops filled with the perfect souvenirs. The marina's many restaurants and bars offer a diverse range of cuisines, ensuring there's something to please every palate. When fun beyond the beach beckons, the marina also boasts a bowling alley, cinema, and playground. And for a true taste of local life, the lively market held every Wednesday and Saturday is a must-visit, where you'll discover locally made products, unique crafts, and clothing.

Island Hopping: Fuerteventura Awaits

Playa Blanca's ferry port serves as your gateway to a day trip adventure. The island of Fuerteventura lies just a 35-minute ferry ride away. Round-trip tickets are easily affordable, and the option to bring a car along lets you explore on your own schedule. Fuerteventura, the Canary Islands' second-largest island, is famed for its expansive beaches, stunning natural parks, and the watersports opportunities its coast provides. Take a day – or more! – to experience all this neighboring island has to offer, then return to the familiar comforts of Playa Blanca at day's end.

Papagayo Beaches

Along Lanzarote's southeastern edge, a string of beaches collectively known as the Papagayo Beaches awaits. Nestled within the Los Ajaches Natural Monument, a protected landscape sculpted by volcanic forces, these beaches hold the distinction of being considered among the finest in Lanzarote and even the entirety of Spain. Their allure lies in the pristine combination of fine white sand, remarkably clear waters, and breathtaking panoramic views. If you crave a beach experience focused on swimming, snorkeling, sunbathing, and pure relaxation, Papagayo delivers an idyllic escape from the crowds.

There are seven beaches in total, with Playa de Papagayo, Playa de la Cera, and Playa del Pozo holding the most widespread renown. Reaching these secluded slices of paradise requires a bit of an adventurous spirit, as they are accessed via a dirt road and require a small entrance fee (3 euros per vehicle). However, for many, this simply adds to their unspoiled charm. The journey can also be made by bike, on foot, or even by arriving by boat. It's essential to be prepared, as the beaches themselves offer no facilities aside from a small restaurant on Playa de Papagayo. Be sure to pack your own food, plenty of water, and ample sunscreen.

Aqualava Water Park: Splashes and Thrills

For a very different kind of water-filled adventure, Aqualava Water Park delivers family-friendly fun in Playa Blanca. This exciting water park is part of the Relaxia Lanzasur Club hotel complex, however, it welcomes day visitors as well. Thrill-seekers will find a variety of attractions and slides designed to get the adrenaline pumping. Brave the Magma River, feel the heat of the Timan Fire, or navigate the twists of Corsario Bay. Little ones have their own dedicated area with a splash zone, a whimsical pirate ship, and a mini slide perfect for pint-sized adventurers. When it's time to refuel, the water park offers a restaurant, snack bar, and shop, and lockers are available for storing your belongings.

One of the unique features of Aqualava is its commitment to sustainability; the water in its many pools is heated through geothermal energy. The park welcomes visitors year-round, with a one-day ticket price of roughly 20 euros for adults and 15 euros for children.

Venturing into Puerto del Carmen

Puerto del Carmen, nestled along Lanzarote's southeastern coastline, draws visitors with its expansive beach, enticing shopping opportunities, and a plethora of exciting activities. Conveniently located a mere 10 kilometers from the airport, and 15 kilometers from the bustling capital of Arrecife, Puerto del Carmen has something for every type of traveler.

Playa Grande: A Beach for Every Mood

The heart of Puerto del Carmen's appeal is undoubtedly Playa Grande. This seemingly endless stretch of golden sand runs for a remarkable 6 kilometers along the town's main promenade, Avenida de las Playas. Clear blue waters make it a haven for swimmers, sunbathers, and those who simply want to relax with the sound of the waves as their soundtrack. Necessary amenities like sunbeds, umbrellas, showers, toilets, and lifeguards ensure comfort and safety.

Playa Grande's impressive length means it offers a variety of experiences depending on which section you choose. Playa de los Pocillos, the easternmost expanse, provides a quieter, more spacious feel, backed by the natural beauty of sand dunes. Nearby Playa de Matagorda is also tranquil and ideal for families, with a small shopping center easily accessible. For those seeking the liveliest atmosphere, head to Playa de Guacimeta, the central and busiest section. Here, the promenade bustles with bars, restaurants, and shops. The more secluded Playa de Los Fariones lies to the west. Its smaller size and rocky areas provide a change of scenery and excellent snorkeling opportunities.

Shopper's Delight
Puerto del Carmen caters to the urge to shop, with choices to suit every style and budget. For a modern mall experience, the Biosfera Plaza Shopping and Leisure Centre is a must-visit. Perched on a hill with sweeping

views of the town and sea, this elegant complex boasts over 50 stores filled with fashion, electronics, cosmetics – and even a supermarket for practical needs. When it's time for a break, the cinema, bowling alley, or tempting food court provide diversions, and the rooftop terrace offers breathtaking panoramas.

The Old Town Harbour exudes a different kind of charm. Here, you'll find traditional products perfect for bringing home a taste of Lanzarote, including local cheeses, honey, wine, and unique souvenirs. The weekly market, held every Friday, is a lively place to pick up fresh seafood, produce, and handcrafted treasures.

Of course, the main promenade, Avenida de las Playas, is lined with still more shops, cafes, and lively bars. Browse for clothing, accessories, jewelry, and gifts. Then, savor a coffee, delicious snack, or a refreshing drink at one of the many inviting terraces.

Activities for Every Interest

Puerto del Carmen ensures there's always something to do – both in and out of the water. Divers flock to this town, drawn by the promise of some of Lanzarote's best dive sites. Playa Chica, the Wreck of the Tiñosa, and the Veril de la Tiñosa offer the chance to encounter an abundance of marine life, from colorful fish and octopus to graceful rays and sea turtles. You might even explore underwater caves, tunnels, and shipwrecks! Numerous dive centers and schools provide everything from equipment rental to lessons and guided tours for divers of every experience level.

If your idea of paradise involves pristine greens, Puerto del Carmen delivers with two nearby golf courses. Both the Lanzarote Golf Resort and the Costa Teguise Golf Club offer stunning 18-hole courses with views of the mountains and coastline. Clubhouses with restaurants and shops provide the perfect place to unwind after a day on the course.

For a fun-filled family outing, Rancho Texas delivers wild animal encounters and aquatic thrills. Crocodiles, tigers, parrots, and sea lions are just a few of the residents you'll meet at this popular animal park. Shows, activities, and attractions add to the excitement. And when it's time to cool off, Rancho Texas also boasts a water park with slides, pools, and kid-friendly splash zones.

Roaming Around Teguise

Teguise: Echoes of the Past

Located in the heart of Lanzarote, Teguise stands as a testament to the island's extensive history. For over 450 years, it proudly served as Lanzarote's capital. Today, it is widely considered one of the most charming and historic towns in the entire Canary Island chain. Within Teguise, remnants of various cultures and eras intertwine to create a unique tapestry of architectural and artistic heritage.

Teguise's Historic Center

The historic center of Teguise has been officially designated an architectural-historical-artistic site, a testament to the numerous buildings and monuments of immense beauty and historical significance found within its boundaries. A leisurely stroll is the perfect way to immerse yourself in the town's rich past. Start with the magnificent Church of Nuestra Señora de Guadalupe. Dating back to the 16th century, with renovations completed in the 18th, its Baroque facade draws the eye while its interior boasts a Mudejar ceiling and a Gothic altarpiece. The church also houses a remarkable assemblage of religious artworks, including paintings, sculptures, and intricate silverwork.

For a glimpse into Lanzarote's efforts to defend itself against marauding pirates, a visit to the Castle of Santa Barbara is essential. Constructed atop the Guanapay volcano in the 16th century, the fortress commands breathtaking panoramic views of both the island and the surrounding sea. Within its walls, the Museum of Piracy delves into the fascinating and sometimes brutal history of piracy in the Canary Islands, showcasing artifacts that bring those tales to life.

The Palacio Spínola provides a window into the lives of Lanzarote's elite. This 18th-century palace was once home to the influential Spínola family. The structure is a stunning example of traditional Canarian architecture, complete with a central courtyard, intricately carved wooden balcony, and beautiful tiled roof. Today, the Palacio Spínola houses the Timple House Museum, a celebration of the timple – a small, guitar-like instrument synonymous with the Canary Islands.

Conclude your tour of the historic center at the 16th-century Convent of San Francisco. Its understated elegance is found in the simplicity of its cloister, church, and peaceful garden. Now home to the Museum of Sacred Art, the convent provides a space to admire Teguise's religious and artistic treasures, including paintings, sculptures, and exquisite vestments.

The Teguise Market: A Sunday Tradition
Each Sunday, the historic center of Teguise transforms into a vibrant tapestry of colors and sounds as the weekly market takes over from 9 am to 2 pm. One of the largest

and most beloved markets in the Canary Islands, it draws countless visitors and locals alike. Browse stalls overflowing with handcrafted treasures, unique souvenirs, clothing, delicious local foods, and music. Beyond the opportunity to find the perfect memento of your visit, the market is a chance to experience the energy of Teguise and discover its traditions.

Venturing Beyond Teguise

Teguise's central location makes it an ideal base for exploring other treasures of Lanzarote. Art lovers will be drawn to the César Manrique Foundation. This cultural center was once the home and studio of the renowned artist and architect who left an indelible mark on Lanzarote's landscape. Here, you can view his works, his impressive art collection, and experience his masterful integration of art with the natural world.

Another of Manrique's creations, the Jardin de Cactus, is a must-visit for any botanical enthusiast. This unique garden is home to over 10,000 cacti from every corner of the globe. Marvel at the astounding variety of shapes, colors, and sizes, with a traditional windmill and volcanic backdrop completing the scene.

For a very different landscape, head to Famara Beach on Lanzarote's northwest coast. This secluded stretch of golden sand and clear blue water is framed by dramatic cliffs and mountains. Whether you choose to relax in the sunshine, swim, or try your hand at surfing, kite-surfing, or hang-gliding, Famara Beach offers an unforgettable escape.

Exploring Other Notable Towns and Villages
Yaiza: A Vision of Tranquility

Nestled in southern Lanzarote, near the otherworldly landscapes of Timanfaya National Park, lies the picturesque town of Yaiza. Often lauded as one of the most beautiful towns in all of Spain, its charm lies in the preservation of traditional architecture. Imagine whitewashed houses adorned with bursts of colorful flowers and adorned by swaying palm trees. A church, museum, and inviting plaza provide places to linger and admire the views that encompass both mountains and the sparkling sea. Yaiza offers a peaceful respite where you can savor the natural beauty and unhurried pace of island life.

El Golfo: Where Colors Collide
The fishing village of El Golfo graces Lanzarote's western coastline and is renowned for a truly unique natural wonder: the Green Lagoon. Also known as Charco de los Clicos, this small lake rests within a volcanic crater. Its vivid green hue, a result of algae and minerals within the water, stands in breathtaking contrast to the black sand of the surrounding beach and the deep blue of the ocean. El Golfo is also home to a beach, a harbor, and a collection of inviting restaurants. These establishments provide the ideal setting for savoring the freshest of seafood and perhaps a glass of the island's renowned wine.

Arrieta: A Surfer's Paradise
On Lanzarote's eastern shore, you'll discover the coastal village of Arrieta. This laid-back spot has a strong draw for surfers and beachcombers enticed by Playa de la

Garita, a generous stretch of sand lapped by clear water with moderate waves perfect for those eager to try their hand at riding the surf. A pier, playground, and a delightful promenade provide places to stroll and take in the views. Arrieta's atmosphere is vibrant and welcoming, with colorful traditional houses, fishing boats, and even the occasional splash of street art adding to its allure.

Orzola: Gateway to La Graciosa

The remote village of Orzola marks Lanzarote's northernmost point, a place where the island seems to simply disappear into the ocean. It is from here that ferries depart to the neighboring island of La Graciosa – the smallest and arguably the most enchanting of the Canary Islands. Orzola itself boasts several beaches perfect for swimming, snorkeling, or simply basking in the sunshine. These include Playa de la Canteria, Playa del Caleton Blanco, and Playa de los Caletones. When hunger strikes, Orzola has a few restaurants eager to tempt you with the local specialty: sancocho canario, a flavorful fish stew served with potatoes and spicy mojo sauce.

Tinajo

Venturing into Lanzarote's interior, you'll find the town of Tinajo. Surrounded by volcanic landscapes and fields dedicated to agriculture, it is here that you can experience a more traditional, authentic way of life on the island. Tinajo's church, museum, and local market offer tastes of the town's heritage, with the market being a particularly good place to find locally produced cheeses, honey, and Lanzarote wine. Tinajo's central location also makes it a convenient starting point for excursions to some of the island's most awe-inspiring natural wonders, including Timanfaya National Park, the winemaking region of La Geria, and the magnificent expanse of Famara Beach.

Top Attractions

Timanfaya National Park

Lanzarote's Timanfaya National Park is a testament to the Earth's dynamic nature. A series of volcanic eruptions in the 18th and 19th centuries left an indelible mark on the island. It all began in 1730 when eruptions began that would continue relentlessly for six years. Vast swaths of the island – nearly a quarter of its total landmass – were buried under molten rock, ash, and debris. Villages and farms were destroyed, and the eruptions dramatically altered Lanzarote's climate and vegetation. The name "Timanfaya" comes from one of these affected areas, paying tribute to a local farmer who had called the region home. Today this park, designated a national park in 1974, stands as the only National Park within Spain that is purely geological in nature.

A Geologist's Playground

Encompassing a remarkable 51.07 square kilometers, Timanfaya National Park showcases over 100 volcanic cones and craters. The park's visual impact comes from a mix of lava fields, craters, calderas, and even geysers. The color palette is stark and otherworldly - a mix of black, red, brown, yellow, and even surprising bursts of green paint the landscape. The geological drama isn't just visible to the eye; the ground beneath your feet holds secrets. Just 13 meters below the surface, temperatures can reach an astounding 600°C. Park staff demonstrate this phenomenon by pouring water into the ground, which instantly transforms into a geyser of steam. Harnessing this heat in a more practical way, there's even a barbecue powered entirely by the volcano's warmth.

Life Finds a Way

The harsh conditions created by Timanfaya's volcanic origins mean plant life is sparse. However, evolution is a powerful force, and certain species have found ways to adapt. Lichens, mosses, succulents, and hardy shrubs tenaciously cling to life within the park's boundaries. The fauna is similarly limited yet includes some endemic species found nowhere else on Earth. Insects, reptiles, birds, and mammals all find niches within the volcanic environment. Perhaps the park's most iconic resident is the

Jameito. This tiny crab, both albino and blind, calls the saltwater lake within the Jameos del Agua caves home. Just offshore, a marine reserve protects the vibrant marine life thriving along the coast.

Experiencing Timanfaya

As one of Lanzarote's most popular tourist destinations, Timanfaya National Park welcomes over a million visitors each year. There are several ways to experience the wonders of this fiery landscape:

- The Ruta de los Volcanes (Volcano Route): This guided bus tour is included in the park entrance fee and lasts approximately 40 minutes. It takes visitors to some of the most breathtaking spots, including the Montañas del Fuego (Mountains of Fire), Islote de Hilario, and Caldera del Corazoncillo.
- Echadero de Camellos (Camel Ride): For a truly memorable way to explore Timanfaya, hop onto the back of a camel. These 20-minute rides take you along the volcanic slopes, offering stunning vistas of the park and glimpses of the coastline. Camels can accommodate two people and cost 12 euros.

- Sendero de Tremensana (Tremensana Trail): Put on your walking shoes and experience Timanfaya on foot with this guided trek. The trail covers roughly 2 kilometers, leading you past lava fields, craters, and cones. These walks are free but be sure to reserve your place in advance at the Visitor Center in Mancha Blanca.
- Sendero de la Costa (Coastal Trail): This 8-kilometer self-guided walk takes you along the park's dramatic coastline, with cliffs, caves, and beaches to discover. No reservation is necessary, and there's no fee to enjoy this walk.

Jameos del Agua: Unique Underground Caves

Lanzarote's Jameos del Agua is a captivating natural phenomenon transformed into a truly unique experience. Formed by eruptions of the Corona Volcano, these caves are part of an immense underground lava tube known as the Tunnel of Atlantis. This subterranean marvel stretches for a remarkable 6 kilometers. The name "Jameos del Agua" references both the large openings found in lava tubes (jameo) and the presence of a mesmerizing saltwater lake within the caves, fed by the ocean itself.

Descending into a Masterpiece

Your journey into the Jameos del Agua begins by descending a staircase into the Jameo Chico, the first and most compact of the cave spaces. Here, you'll encounter a ticket office, souvenir shop, and a bar offering refreshments. This space is where the influence of Lanzarote's beloved artist and architect, César Manrique, becomes apparent. His vision transformed these caves into a welcoming space, seamlessly integrating natural volcanic rock, plants, and wood to create a harmonious environment. Manrique's artistic touch is also evidenced in sculptures, paintings, and thoughtfully placed lighting that enhances the beauty of the caves.

The Lake: Heart of the Caves

A narrow tunnel links the Jameo Chico to the Jameo Grande, the most expansive of the caves and home to the Jameos del Agua's most celebrated feature: the subterranean saltwater lake. Stretching roughly 100 meters long with varying depths, the lake shimmers with a captivating turquoise hue created by sunlight and the unique minerals in the water. But the lake's beauty isn't simply visual; it is home to a unique and fascinating creature called the jameito. These endemic squat lobsters, small, white, and blind, are found exclusively in this lake and other sections of the lava tube. The jameitos are incredibly sensitive to their environment, making their protection crucial. Remember, it's strictly forbidden to touch the water or toss anything into the lake.

Dining Underground

On the far side of the lake, you'll find a restaurant integrated seamlessly into the cave itself. Enjoy salads, soups, meats, fish, desserts, and a range of beverages – all with a breathtaking view of the lake thanks to a large window. If the weather is fine, opt for the terrace with its open-air vistas. On certain evenings (Tuesdays, Fridays, and Saturdays), the restaurant's stage comes alive with music or other performances.

Garden Oasis and Volcanic Exploration

Exiting the restaurant, you'll discover a tranquil garden. Palm trees, vibrant flowers, and cacti create a burst of life in contrast to the cave's volcanic heart. The garden's focal point is a shimmering emerald-green pool with a gently bubbling fountain – another example of Manrique's artistic vision blending water elements with the raw power of volcanic rock. You'll also find a viewpoint within the garden, ideal for soaking up panoramic views of the coastline and Lanzarote's mountainous terrain.

The final cave, the Jameo de la Cazuela, houses a museum dedicated to the science behind Lanzarote's volcanic origins. Called the Casa de los Volcanes, its exhibits include engaging displays, models, maps, videos, and even virtual reality experiences designed to explain how the island and its volcanoes were formed. You'll find a laboratory demonstrating instruments used to monitor ongoing volcanic and seismic activity, and a library filled with resources for those eager to deepen their knowledge of geology and volcanology.

César Manrique Foundation

Lanzarote's unique beauty and character are forever intertwined with the life and works of César Manrique.

This visionary, born in 1919, dedicated his life to creating a harmonious blend between the island's natural wonders and the built environment. His artistic creations, from the Jameos del Agua to the Jardín de Cactus, have become iconic symbols of Lanzarote. Sadly, Manrique passed away in 1992, but his mission to preserve Lanzarote's identity and respect its environment lives on through the César Manrique Foundation.

The Foundation

Located in the small town of Tahíche, within the municipality of Teguise, the César Manrique Foundation is both a cultural center and a popular tourist destination. For 20 years, from 1968 to 1988, Tahíche was Manrique's home and base of operations. The foundation itself is housed within a remarkable dwelling designed by Manrique, a testament to his ability to seamlessly meld natural and man-made elements. Local volcanic rock, vibrant plants, and wood are integrated into a structure that makes ingenious use of a lava field left behind by 18th-century eruptions. The home is built on two levels. The upper level reflects traditional Canarian architecture, with crisp white walls, green-trimmed windows, and a warm tiled roof. Contrasting with this is the lower level, carved directly into the lava rock. A series of interconnected rooms and tunnels create a fascinating subterranean space within the dwelling.

Manrique's artistic spirit permeates this unique home. Paintings, sculptures, and objects he created throughout his life reside alongside works by other renowned artists, including Picasso, Miró, and Tapies.

Exploring the Foundation

The César Manrique Foundation offers visitors a variety of ways to fully immerse themselves in its offerings:

- The Volcano House: The heart of the foundation, this is the dwelling Manrique himself built upon the lava field. Wandering through the Volcano House, you gain insight into both his personal life and his artistic process. The living room, dining room, kitchen, bedroom, and studio all offer unique glimpses into the mind of the artist. You'll encounter Manrique's work and collections throughout the house. Don't miss the pool, barbecue, and lush garden –

more examples of integrating nature into the living space. Perhaps the most breathtaking feature is a panoramic window that frames stunning views of the lava landscape and the ocean beyond.

- The Art Gallery: The room that once served as Manrique's personal studio has been transformed into a gallery showcasing his paintings. Here, you'll find works by other notable artists displayed as well, such as Luis Feito, Gerardo Rueda, and Manuel Rivera. The diverse collection spans styles from colorful abstracts to monochrome figuration, geometric to organic. Natural light floods the space thanks to a thoughtfully placed skylight.
- The Sculpture Garden: Enveloping the Volcano House, the Sculpture Garden showcases an array of works by Manrique and his contemporaries. Metal, stone, and wood take shape as sculptures both large and small, complex and simple, realistic and abstract. Artists like Eduardo Chillida, Martín Chirino, and Eusebio Sempere are also represented here. A fountain, pond, and the gentle turning of a windmill create a tranquil atmosphere within the garden.

- The Library: This dedicated space houses an impressive collection exceeding 10,000 volumes. The focus is on works related to Manrique, his art, and broader topics such as art, culture, and the natural world. Works in a variety of languages, from Spanish to English, cover topics as diverse as literature, history, science, and philosophy. The library provides both a reading room for leisurely perusal of the collection and a computer room where visitors can tap into the foundation's digital archive.

The César Manrique Foundation welcomes visitors daily and charges a modest entrance fee. Beyond self-exploration, the foundation offers guided tours and hosts diverse events like workshops, concerts, and conferences, all aimed at celebrating Manrique's legacy. A visit isn't complete without stopping by the shop, where you'll find a tempting selection of souvenirs, books, and other items connected to Manrique and his inspirational body of work.

Famara Beach: Surfing Paradise

Located on Lanzarote's northwest coast, near the town of Caleta de Famara, lies Famara Beach (also known as Playa de Famara). With its expanse of golden sand, crystal-clear turquoise waters, and a dramatic backdrop formed by cliffs and mountains, Famara consistently ranks among the most beautiful beaches in Lanzarote and throughout Spain. But for surfers, Famara holds a special allure – it's an undisputed paradise for those who love riding the waves. The beach is part of the Natural Park of the Chinijo Archipelago, ensuring its wild beauty remains unspoiled.

Why Surfers Flock to Famara

Famara Beach boasts a unique combination of natural features that make it a haven for surfers of all skill levels. The consistency of the swell, a sandy ocean bottom, and a wide, lengthy shore break provide the perfect playground for learning the sport or honing your existing skills. The variety of waves is another major draw. Depending on factors like the tide, wind, and season, you'll encounter everything from gentle rollers perfect for beginners to powerful waves that challenge even seasoned surfers. The beach has a designated surf zone, clearly marked with flags and buoys. This ensures those focused on catching waves can do so freely without encroaching on those simply enjoying a swim or other water activities.

The infrastructure of Famara supports its reputation as a surfer's mecca. Numerous surf schools and shops mean you'll find everything you need, whether you're a novice who needs lessons and equipment rentals or a seasoned surfer seeking expert guidance or gear for purchase. Here's just a small sampling of the established businesses ready to meet your surfing needs:

- Famara Surf: This combination surf school and shop caters to everyone from those taking their first tentative steps on a board to those yearning to improve their technique. Experienced, qualified instructors tailor lessons to your individual skill level for a safe and enjoyable experience. And, of course, the shop offers a wide variety of surfboards, wetsuits, and accessories.

- Red Star Surf: Another excellent choice, Red Star Surf's focus is on providing a welcoming and relaxed atmosphere for surfers of every level. Their professional instructors can take you to the island's best breaks and offer guidance perfectly suited to help you progress. Red Star also offers camps, providing an immersive surf experience. Like most in the region, they also have a shop stocked with surfboards, clothing, and souvenirs.
- Lanzasurf: The passionate instructors at Lanzasurf are certified and committed to creating a supportive learning environment. They offer courses and retreats and even have rental options, meaning you can try out different boards to find your perfect fit. And, for those necessary supplies and fun souvenirs, be sure to check out their shop.

Beyond the Surf

While Famara Beach holds the title of surfing paradise, it's far from a one-trick pony. There are plenty of ways to experience the beauty and energy of this special place.

- Kite-surfing: Harness the power of the wind that also draws surfers to Famara by trying your hand at kite-surfing! The steady breezes create ideal conditions for this exhilarating sport. Imagine soaring above the waves, mastering jumps, and performing thrilling tricks – all while soaking in breathtaking views of the beach and cliffs. Need gear or lessons? Several established businesses cater to kite-surfers, including Famara Kite School, Kite Center Lanzarote, and Kite Surfing Lanzarote.

- Hiking: Discover the wild beauty of Famara and its surrounding landscape on foot. The beach itself provides miles of sand for leisurely walks, or, for more of a challenge, tackle the cliffs for panoramic vistas. Venturing inland, you might explore nearby villages and immerse yourself in the unique flora, fauna, and geological wonders of the area. For those who prefer a guided experience, options like the Famara Cliff Hike, Famara Beach Hike, or Famara Sunset Hike offer a range of routes, difficulty levels, and the benefit of commentary from knowledgeable local guides.
- Paragliding: For the ultimate adrenaline rush and a truly unique perspective on Famara Beach, take to the skies with a paragliding adventure! Whether you choose a solo flight (experience required) or opt for the tandem

experience, you'll feel the freedom of soaring above the beach, cliffs, and surrounding landscape. Companies like Lanzarote Paragliding, Parapente Lanzarote, and Paragliding Lanzarote are ready to provide equipment and lessons, or simply arrange an unforgettable flight experience.

Amenities for Visitors

Famara Beach strives to ensure visitors have everything they need for a comfortable and enjoyable day. Parking is a breeze, with multiple free lots located both along the beachfront and within the town itself. Keep in mind weekends and holidays tend to be busiest, so either arrive early or consider utilizing public transportation to avoid the crowds. You'll find showers and clean restrooms located near the entrance of the beach, within the designated surf zone. They are open from 10 am to 6 pm and are free to use (just bring your own towel and toiletries). Lifeguards and security personnel are a reassuring presence, particularly during the busiest seasons and times of day. They provide an extra layer of safety, first aid, and assistance if needed. And when it's time for a break, Famara has you covered with a variety of restaurants and bars scattered along the beach and within the town. Fresh seafood, pizza, burgers, salads, refreshing beverages, coffee – you'll find something to satisfy your cravings. Establishments like Restaurante El Sol, Restaurante El Risco, and Bar La Esquina are popular spots to refuel and unwind while enjoying the seaside ambiance.

Mirador del Río: Spectacular Viewpoint

Perched atop the Risco de Famara, a dramatic 500-meter high cliff on Lanzarote's northern coast, sits the spectacular Mirador del Río. This remarkable viewpoint, born from the brilliant mind of César Manrique, is a testament to his ability to seamlessly blend the built environment with the stunning natural landscape of his beloved island. The municipality of Haría, located roughly 25 kilometers from the capital of Arrecife, is home to this architectural gem.

The Mirador del Río's history began in the early 1970s. The site once held a 19th-century military battery, and it was this abandoned structure that Manrique ingeniously repurposed. His work made use of local volcanic rock, plants, and wood – materials that would become hallmarks of his architectural creations. But perhaps most striking is how he integrated the building into its clifftop setting, rendering it almost invisible from afar. This integration epitomizes Manrique's deep respect for Lanzarote's landscape and his desire to create structures that complemented rather than competed with nature.

A View Like No Other

Words hardly do justice to the breathtaking panorama that awaits visitors to the Mirador del Río. It is often called one of the most spectacular views in Lanzarote, if not the entire Canary Island chain. Your gaze will be drawn to the Chinijo Archipelago, a cluster of small islands protected as a Natural Park. La Graciosa, the archipelago's only inhabited island, is the largest. The others include Alegranza, Montaña Clara, Roque del Este, and Roque del Oeste. Below, the majestic Risco de Famara, its striated cliffs showcasing a myriad of colors and textures, stretches along Lanzarote's western coast. The narrow strait of water separating Lanzarote from La Graciosa, called El Río, lends its name to the viewpoint itself. The magic here reaches its peak at sunrise and sunset, when the interplay of light and shadow transforms the vista into a living canvas.

Amenities to Enhance Your Visit

The Mirador del Río isn't simply about the view. It offers a range of thoughtful amenities to ensure a comfortable and memorable visit. Enjoy a snack, meal, or refreshing drink at the cafeteria, where floor-to-ceiling windows offer stunning views of the sea and islands. If the weather permits, opt for the terrace, where you can soak up the sunshine while admiring the cliffs and mountains. The cafeteria serves up a selection of sandwiches, salads, cakes, and beverages like coffee, tea, and wine. Of course, no visit would be complete without a stop at the souvenir shop. Postcards, magnets, keychains, t-shirts, mugs, and books related to both the Mirador del Río and César Manrique are all available for purchase. The shop even has a special display showcasing Manrique's artistic works, including paintings, sculptures, and posters. Ample parking is available near the viewpoint's entrance, and, thankfully, there's no fee to park. Be aware that weekends and holidays can get crowded, so arriving early or opting for public transport is wise on those days.

The Mirador del Río welcomes visitors daily and charges a modest entrance fee. They also host a variety of activities and events, from guided tours that delve into Manrique's work to concerts and exhibitions. All these serve to further illuminate the legacy of this remarkably talented artist. For more information or to book your tickets in advance, be sure to visit the Mirador del Río website.

Cactus Garden: Botanical Wonder

The Cactus Garden, also known as Jardín de Cactus, was the final creation of Lanzarote's beloved and visionary artist, César Manrique. Completed in the early 1990s, this unique garden was built on the site of an abandoned quarry. The quarry had provided volcanic sand lapilli, known locally as "picón" or "rofe," which was used agriculturally to help retain moisture in the soil. With his characteristic respect for Lanzarote's landscape, Manrique envisioned transforming this industrial space into a place of beauty, paying homage to a plant he deeply admired: the cactus. To ensure the botanical aspect of the project was executed with the utmost care, Manrique collaborated with botanist Estanislao González Ferrer in the selection and arrangement of the plants.

Design and Diversity

The Cactus Garden boasts a circular design, measuring 50 meters across and with a depth of 15 meters. This meticulously structured space has the capacity to house a staggering 10,000 cacti! The plants belong to an impressive 450 species encompassing 13 different families and hail from all five continents. The garden is built on multiple levels, terraces, and paths, creating a visually engaging and dynamic experience. At the garden's center stands a traditional windmill, meticulously restored, providing a striking contrast to the surrounding cacti and volcanic rock. This windmill is a nod to Lanzarote's history; it was once used to grind cochineal insects, from which a valuable natural dye was produced. You'll also find a water feature – a fountain that adds another textural element to this celebration of nature. The garden's overall design is clean and minimalist, relying heavily on Lanzarote's natural materials like volcanic rock, local plants, and wood. The artistic touch of Manrique is evident in sculptures, paintings, and thoughtfully placed lighting that add another dimension to the garden's atmosphere.

Amenities to Enhance Your Experience
The Cactus Garden goes beyond the plants themselves, offering amenities that make a visit both enjoyable and convenient. Take a break to refuel at the cafeteria, where you can enjoy snacks, meals, or drinks while taking in the view of the garden and the surrounding cochineal fields. Floor-to-ceiling windows and an outdoor terrace provide a choice of viewing spots. Naturally, the Cactus Garden has a well-stocked souvenir shop. Browse for postcards, magnets, t-shirts, and a variety of other items celebrating

both the garden and the works of César Manrique. The shop also showcases a collection of Manrique's paintings, sculptures, and posters. Parking at the garden is convenient and free, although weekends and holidays do get crowded so consider arriving early or using public transportation.

The Cactus Garden welcomes visitors daily and charges a reasonable entrance fee. They also host events like guided tours, concerts, and exhibitions – all designed to introduce more people to Manrique's legacy and vision. For additional information or to book your tickets in advance, visit the Cactus Garden website.

El Golfo: Green Lagoon and Black Sand Beach

The picturesque fishing village of El Golfo is nestled along Lanzarote's western coastline. This place owes its very existence to the island's volcanic past. A series of eruptions between 1730 and 1736 dramatically reshaped the landscape, with nearly a quarter of Lanzarote buried in ash, rock, and newly created lava flows. Villages and farmland were lost, and the climate and vegetation of the island underwent a permanent transformation. The name "El Golfo" references the fact that the lava flow reached the ocean, carving out a bay or gulf along the coast. And it is within this bay that El Golfo's most iconic feature, the Green Lagoon, was created. Ocean water infiltrated the volcanic crater, and over time, its interaction with the minerals resulted in the formation of this unique lake. It's also known as Charco de los Clicos – a name derived from a type of shellfish once plentiful in the lagoon whose existence was tragically cut short by a pair of introduced turtles. The final piece of this geological puzzle is the black sand beach, a product of the relentless forces of wind and water eroding the volcanic rock.

El Golfo: A Popular Destination

Understandably, El Golfo is a major draw for visitors to Lanzarote, with thousands flocking to the village every year. Here's what you can expect to find:

- The Green Lagoon: This captivating natural feature is the star attraction of El Golfo and instantly recognizable in photos of Lanzarote. A short, two-minute walk from the village brings you to the lagoon, which nestles within a small bay. A wooden fence surrounds it, underscoring its protected status as a natural reserve. Swimming and even touching the water are strictly forbidden to ensure the lagoon's delicate ecosystem remains undisturbed. But a designated viewpoint affords breathtaking vistas where the vivid green of the lake, the deep black of the sand, and the azure of the ocean collide in a symphony of colors. Film buffs may recognize the lagoon, as it was featured in the 1966 movie "One Million Years B.C." starring Raquel Welch.

- The Black Sand Beach: El Golfo's other major draw is its unique black sand beach, one of the few on Lanzarote. Located on the opposite side of the Green Lagoon, it's accessible via a simple dirt path. While this beach isn't ideal for swimming due to strong waves, currents, and the lack of lifeguards, it's a wonderful place to stroll, sunbathe, and simply soak in the dramatic views of the cliffs and endless ocean. You'll also find a natural pool – a refreshing spot to cool off and perhaps observe the sea life trapped by the tides.

- Restaurants and Bars: After exploring the natural wonders, El Golfo offers authentic dining experiences showcasing the freshest of seafood and local flavors. The village boasts several restaurants and bars strung along the coast, each with its own inviting ambiance. Sample delicious fish soup, perfectly grilled fish, paella, or the Canary Islands specialty sancocho canario – a hearty stew of fish, potatoes, and the traditional mojo sauce. No meal here is complete without a glass of Lanzarote's distinctive wine, made from the malvasia grape that thrives in the volcanic soil. Restaurante El Golfo, Restaurante Mar Azul, and Bar La Piscina are just a few of the establishments ready to satisfy your appetite.

Outdoor Activities

Hiking and Trekking Trails

Caldera Blanca

One of Lanzarote's most beloved hikes centers around Caldera Blanca. This immense volcanic crater, measuring 1.2 kilometers across and 200 meters deep, is part of Timanfaya National Park and is a testament to the eruptions of 1730. Your hike begins in the village of Mancha Blanca. From there, a combination of dirt roads and clear paths will lead you through a landscape sculpted by volcanic forces: lava fields, smaller cones, and tenacious plant life. The hike is considered moderately challenging due to some steep sections and loose rocks, but it's suitable for most fitness levels. The roughly 9.3-kilometer trek takes approximately 3 hours. The reward for your efforts comes once you reach the crater's rim. The panoramic vistas are simply breathtaking, encompassing neighboring volcanoes, sparkling ocean, and even the island of La Graciosa.

Camino de los Gracioseros

If your idea of the perfect hike includes a hefty dose of challenge that culminates at a secluded beach, then the Camino de los Gracioseros is for you. Starting in the village of Yé, you'll embark on a steep and narrow trail that descends from the top of the Risco de Famara – a cliff soaring 500 meters high – to the valley below. Good physical condition and solid hiking skills are non-negotiable on this trail, and those with a fear of heights may want to skip this one. The total trek covers about 6 kilometers and takes roughly 2 hours. The prize at the end is El Risco beach, a pristine strip of sand accessible only on foot or by boat. Here, you can swim, sunbathe, and simply savor the quiet beauty of your surroundings. You'll also be treated to views of the Chinijo Archipelago, a cluster of small islands holding protected Natural Park status.

Monte Corona

For a mix of geological interest and sweeping views, Monte Corona is a great option. This volcano, formed some 20,000 years ago, stands 609 meters high, making it

Lanzarote's highest point. This hike also begins in Yé, and you'll initially follow paved roads that give way to dirt tracks as you ascend through fields, vineyards, and groves of palm trees. Difficulty-wise, this hike is considered relatively easy, with a gentle slope and a well-defined path. Do be prepared for wind and potentially cool temperatures at the summit. The 4.2-kilometer hike shouldn't take more than an hour. Once you reach the top, the reward isn't just bragging rights – you'll be treated to a 360-degree panorama of the entire island, the ocean, and neighboring islands like La Graciosa, Alegranza, and Montaña Clara.

Los Ajaches

The Los Ajaches Natural Monument provides a stunning backdrop for a hike that showcases the wild beauty of Lanzarote's south. This volcanic formation covers a vast area and is roughly 15 million years old. Expect a variety of terrain as you traverse hills, valleys, cliffs, and even encounter a few beaches. The starting point for this hike is the village of Femés. Cobbled paths and dirt roads will lead you through highlights like the Barranco de la

Higuera, the Pico de la Aceituna, and the Degollada de Carlos. Some sections are steep and rocky, making this trek moderately difficult. It covers approximately 7 kilometers and takes about 2.5 hours to complete. Make the effort, and you'll be met with incredible vistas of coastline, ocean, and the islands of Fuerteventura and Lobos.

Cycling Routes

La Graciosa: A Cyclist's Paradise

If a cycling adventure that includes a ferry ride and an island with no cars sounds appealing, then La Graciosa is the route for you. Start in the village of Orzola, where ferries depart for La Graciosa, the smallest and arguably most charming of the Canary Islands. It's also part of the Chinijo Archipelago Natural Park. The ferry takes a mere 30 minutes and will set you back around 20 euros for a round-trip ticket. Once on La Graciosa, you'll discover it's a haven for cyclists. Dirt roads and trails connect villages, beaches, and viewpoints. You won't encounter any paved roads or car traffic – just the occasional jeep and plenty of fellow cyclists. The island's flat terrain makes it a welcoming choice for cyclists of all abilities, including families. The full route covers about 21 kilometers and should take roughly 2 hours. Here's what you can expect along the way:

- Caleta del Sebo: This is the island's primary village and port. Here, you'll find the ferry terminal and essential services like a supermarket, pharmacy, and tourist office. Crucially, this is also where you'll find bike rental shops! Expect to pay around 10 euros to rent a bike for the day. (You can bring your own for a small surcharge on the ferry).
- Montaña del Mojón: If you enjoy a climb, put this 188-meter peak on your itinerary. It's the highest point on La Graciosa. The path to the summit is steep and rocky, but the panoramic views of the island and ocean make it worthwhile. Look for the lighthouse, windmill, and cross that stand proudly at the top.
- Las Agujas: This trio of small islands just off the coast of La Graciosa falls within the protected natural park. The best place to glimpse them is from Playa de las Conchas, considered one of La Graciosa's most stunning and

secluded beaches. The combination of golden sand, clear turquoise water, and the dramatic mountain and cliff backdrop is unforgettable. While the beach is inviting for swimming, snorkeling, or surfing, be aware of the strong waves and currents.

Timanfaya National Park

For a glimpse into the volcanic forces that shaped Lanzarote, embark on a cycling route through Timanfaya National Park. This unique and mesmerizing park is undeniably one of the island's biggest draws. Begin your adventure in the village of Yaiza. From there, you'll follow a mix of paved roads and dirt tracks as you traverse lava fields, pass volcanic cones, and push past tenacious vegetation. This route is classified as moderately challenging due to some steep sections and loose rocks, but it's doable for most cyclists with a reasonable fitness level. Expect to spend about 3.5 hours on the bike to complete the roughly 46-kilometer route. Points of interest include:

- Monumento Natural de Montañas de Fuego: This natural monument encompasses an impressive 24 square kilometers and is home to over 100 volcanoes and cones. Born from eruptions between 1730 and 1736, it's a place where the fiery birth of the island is laid bare. The color palette is striking, a mix of black, red, brown, yellow, and green. Perhaps even more surprising is the incredibly high temperature lingering just below the surface. At a depth of a mere 13 meters, the ground can reach a scorching 600°C!

La Geria

The La Geria wine region is another example of how Lanzarote's volcanic past has shaped its present. Covering 52 square kilometers, it is one of the island's most distinctive and iconic landscapes. Here, necessity became the mother of invention, and a unique method of viticulture was born. Individual vines are planted in holes dug directly into the volcanic soil, then covered with volcanic sand called picón. This layer of picón is crucial, helping to retain precious moisture and shielding the grapes from the relentless sun and wind. Stone walls known as "zocos" encircle each hole, adding another layer of protection. The region produces high-quality wine made from the malvasia grape, which flourishes in the fertile volcanic soil. Several wineries dot the region and welcome visitors. Take a tour to see the production process, explore the vineyards, and, of course, sample the wines.

Mirador del Río

If you're an experienced cyclist who relishes a challenge, test your skills on the route leading to the Mirador del Río. This spectacular viewpoint sits atop the Risco de Famara, a dramatic 500-meter cliff on Lanzarote's north coast. Your journey begins in the village of Orzola, with a mix of paved and dirt roads guiding you past fields, vineyards, and groves of palm trees. With steep climbs and sections best suited for those with solid cycling skills, this route isn't for the faint of heart. Those who persevere will be rewarded with breathtaking panoramas of the Chinijo Archipelago and the Risco de Famara itself. The viewpoint, another masterpiece by Lanzarote's beloved César Manrique, was built on the site of a 19th-century military battery. As always, Manrique used natural materials that blend seamlessly with the environment.

From the Mirador del Río, the Chinijo Archipelago, a protected natural park, can be seen in all its glory. The largest and only inhabited island is La Graciosa, with Alegranza, Montaña Clara, Roque del Este, and Roque del Oeste completing the archipelago. Don't miss the cafeteria, where you can refuel while enjoying the views, or the souvenir shop for a memento of your cycling victory.

Monte Corona

Monte Corona stands tall as Lanzarote's highest point, soaring 609 meters above the landscape. This volcano wasn't born yesterday; it was formed during an eruption some 20,000 years ago. That same eruption was responsible for the creation of an impressive 6-kilometer lava tube known as the Tunnel of Atlantis. Within this subterranean wonder, you'll find hidden caves and even lakes. Monte Corona also boasts a crater of considerable size – approximately 250 meters across and with a depth of 80 meters. If you're the adventurous type, lace up your hiking boots and prepare to ascend Monte Corona! The path to the summit is steep and rocky, but the panoramic views are absolutely worth the effort. Imagine standing at the top and taking in the entirety of Lanzarote, the shimmering ocean, and neighboring islands like La Graciosa, Alegranza, and Montaña Clara. And keep your eyes peeled for the lighthouse, windmill, and cross that also mark the summit.

Playa la Caleta: Blissful Beach Relaxation

Sometimes the best experiences are the simplest, and Playa la Caleta exemplifies this perfectly. This secluded stretch of golden sand lies along Lanzarote's east coast, tucked near the village of Arrieta. Picture yourself sinking your toes into the sand and gazing out at clear, azure ocean. The atmosphere here is undeniably tranquil – perfect for swimming, sunbathing, or simply letting the cares of the world melt away. If you're feeling more active, Playa la Caleta is also known for great surfing, kite-surfing, and snorkeling conditions. Those traveling with little ones will appreciate the playground, and the promenade is a lovely place for a leisurely stroll while soaking in the seaside ambiance.

Watersports

Surfing: Catching Waves in Paradise

Lanzarote is a surfer's dream, with a variety of breaks to suit every skill level. Imagine the thrill of riding the waves, feeling the rush of adrenaline, and working to perfect your technique – all while surrounded by breathtaking coastal and volcanic vistas. Numerous surf schools and shops across the island are ready to help you get started or reach that next level. Companies like Lava Flow Surf, Mojo Surf, and Pro Center Antxon Otaegui offer gear rentals, lessons, and even guided tours. Here are a few of Lanzarote's most popular surf spots:

- Famara Beach: Located on the island's northwest coast near the town of Caleta de Famara, this iconic surf beach is part of the Chinijo Archipelago Natural Park. Its expansive sandy beach, clear waters, and moderate waves make it ideal for those new to the sport. But don't be fooled – Famara offers a range of breaks, from gentle rollers to powerful waves suitable for more seasoned surfers. The designated surf zone ensures everyone can enjoy the water safely.

- La Santa: This west-coast surfing mecca near the village of La Santa faces the mighty Atlantic Ocean. It boasts two world-renowned waves – El Quemao and La Derecha. These powerful, fast-breaking waves are strictly for experienced, even professional, surfers. The shallow reef they break over demands respect, but those with the skills to tackle them are in for an unforgettable experience.
- Playa de las Cucharas: Located in the resort town of Costa Teguise on Lanzarote's eastern coast, this beach is known for the reliable trade winds that whip up perfect conditions for windsurfing and kite-surfing. But Playa de las Cucharas also has a regular, fun wave that caters to surfers of all levels, particularly those new to the sport. A buoyed-off surf zone keeps surfers and swimmers safely separated.

Diving

If the world beneath the waves calls to you, Lanzarote's got you covered! The island's clear, warm waters teem with diverse marine life and fascinating volcanic formations. Prepare to discover colorful fish, vibrant coral reefs, mysterious caves and tunnels, and even shipwrecks

– some natural, and some placed intentionally to create artificial reefs. One particularly unique dive takes you to an underwater museum! Companies like Lanzarote Non Stop Divers, Aquasport Diving, and Pura Vida Diving are ready to provide equipment, lessons, and guided excursions suited to your experience level. Here's a peek at one of Lanzarote's top dive sites:

- Playa Chica: This diving paradise lies in the resort of Puerto del Carmen on the island's southeast coast, conveniently located near the airport. Its calm, shallow waters house a variety of sites to explore, making it perfect for everyone from novices to seasoned divers. Expect a remarkable concentration of marine life, with angel sharks, rays, octopus, moray eels, seahorses, and cuttlefish among the species you might encounter. Several artificial reefs, including the wrecks of a tugboat and fishing ship, add to the diversity and provide shelter to even more sea creatures.

Museo Atlántico: A Submerged Masterpiece

The Museo Atlántico, located in the south near the Playa Blanca resort, is unlike any other dive experience. This underwater museum is the brainchild of British artist Jason deCaires Taylor, who's responsible for sculpting over 300 human figures now resting between 12 and 15 meters beneath the surface. The figures are arranged into thought-provoking scenes and installations. The museum's purpose extends beyond creating stunning visuals; it aims to raise awareness of our oceans and inspire respect for marine life. The sculptures also function as an artificial reef, encouraging the growth and proliferation of diverse marine species. The Museo Atlántico is accessible only by boat, and both divers and snorkelers can enjoy the experience with the assistance of a guide.

Los Jameos del Agua

Located in the island's northeast near the village of Arrieta, Los Jameos del Agua offers a dive experience steeped in the island's volcanic history. This natural wonder sits within the Tunnel of Atlantis, a 6-kilometer lava tube formed by eruptions of the Corona Volcano. Within this tube are numerous caves and subterranean lakes interconnected by a network of tunnels. The most renowned is the Jameo del Agua, boasting a mesmerizing saltwater lake with a turquoise hue. Even more captivating are the lake's inhabitants: an endemic and unique species of squat lobster known as the jameito. These small, white, and blind crustaceans are found only in this lake and a few other isolated spots within the lava tube. Their delicate nature means they are protected by law, and the fragile ecosystem makes this dive suitable only for experienced divers with special permits, accompanied by a guide.

Parasailing: Soaring Above the Waves

For a thrilling bird's-eye view of Lanzarote, try your hand at parasailing! Feel the rush of adrenaline as you effortlessly glide through the air, towed behind a boat. Take in the breathtaking volcanic landscapes, vibrant coastline, and endless beaches. You can parasail solo or with a partner and tailor the flight's height and duration to your preferences. Companies like Paracraft Lanzarote, Watersports Lanzarote, and Catlanza stand ready to provide equipment, instruction, and unforgettable flights. Here are a few of Lanzarote's prime locations for parasailing:

- Puerto del Carmen: This bustling resort on the southeast coast is a parasailing hub. Its lively promenade is lined with shops, restaurants, and vibrant beaches boasting golden sands and clear water. The harbor is your launching point for flights over the expansive bay, with panoramic views of the mountains and coastline. Reach heights of up to 80 meters, fly for as long as 10 minutes, and create lasting memories via photos or videos of your adventure.
- Playa Blanca: Experience a different side of Lanzarote with a parasailing flight launched from Playa Blanca. This southern resort boasts a more tranquil vibe, with white-sand beaches, a picturesque marina, and even a fishing port. From high above the water, you'll enjoy stunning vistas of the islands Fuerteventura and Lobos, and perhaps even catch a glimpse of the magnificent Papagayo beaches – renowned for their pristine conditions. Soar up to 100 meters high, enjoy flights of up to 15 minutes, and keep your eyes peeled for dolphins, turtles, and other marine life visible from your lofty vantage point.

Diving and Snorkeling Spots

Playa Chica

Situated on Lanzarote's southeastern coast, in the resort town of Puerto del Carmen, Playa Chica is an underwater wonderland. Its convenient location near the airport makes it an easily accessible option. The calm, shallow waters surrounding its small, sandy beach hold a variety of dive sites catering to both seasoned divers and those just starting their underwater adventures. Prepare to be amazed by the abundance and diversity of marine life; angel sharks, rays, octopus, moray eels, seahorses, and cuttlefish are just a few of the creatures you might encounter. Playa Chica also boasts several artificial reefs, including a fishing boat and tugboat wreck. These intentionally placed structures attract even more marine life, enhancing the diving experience.

Museo Atlántico: Art Meets Conservation

For a dive that's as thought-provoking as it is beautiful, head to the Museo Atlántico off the island's southern coast near Playa Blanca. This underwater museum is the vision of British artist Jason deCaires Taylor. Over 300 of his human figure sculptures rest at a depth of 12 to 15 meters, arranged in evocative scenes. However, the museum's purpose extends beyond the purely artistic. It aims to raise awareness about the importance of ocean conservation and functions as an artificial reef, promoting the proliferation of diverse marine species. The Museo Atlántico is accessible only by boat, and both divers and snorkelers can immerse themselves in this unique experience with the aid of a guide.

Los Jameos del Agua

A truly special dive experience awaits within Los Jameos del Agua, located in the northeast near the village of Arrieta. This site lies within the Tunnel of Atlantis, a 6-kilometer lava tube born from eruptions of the Corona Volcano. A series of caves and subterranean lakes, linked by tunnels, can be explored within the tube. The most awe-inspiring is the Jameo del Agua, where a mesmerizing saltwater lake shimmers with a turquoise hue. Even more fascinating are the lake's inhabitants: the jameito, a unique species of squat lobster. These small, white, and blind crustaceans are found only within this lake and a few other isolated spots within the lava tube. The delicate nature of this ecosystem means diving here is restricted to experienced divers who have secured a special permit and will be accompanied by a guide.

Veril de Playa Chica

The Veril de Playa Chica, situated on Lanzarote's southeastern coast, is considered the island's premier snorkeling and diving destination. A sandy platform known as the "Veril of Playa Chica" creates extensive shallow areas perfect for those new to snorkeling. Depths near the shore average around 10 meters, with crystal clear, calm waters ensuring excellent visibility. The presence of wave-blocking barriers contributes to the tranquility. This protected environment is a haven for marine life. Expect to encounter vibrantly colored crustaceans, octopus, cuttlefish, and perhaps even a shark. Venture towards the moored boats, and you might be rewarded with the sight of seahorses nestled amongst the ropes.

Playa Flamingo

Located in the southern resort town of Playa Blanca, Playa Flamingo is a 250-meter stretch of beach sheltered by breakwaters. These barriers create a calm oasis, making it a perfect spot for snorkelers of all levels, even young children. Inside the breakwaters, you'll discover plentiful fish to observe. But the real adventure lies beyond the barrier, where you may cross paths with barracuda, tuna, or even vast schools of sardines.

Playa del Jablillo

On Lanzarote's eastern coast, within the resort of Costa Teguise, lies Playa del Jablillo. Its sheltered artificial bay boasts calm, safe waters perfect for those just starting their snorkeling adventures. Prepare to be dazzled by schools of colorful fish, including dreamfish, bream, seabream, and tiny damselfish. Exotic wrasses with their vibrant hues add to the visual feast. Even spider crabs, wide-eyed flounder, and stingrays call this protected bay home.

Camel Rides and Jeep Safaris

Camel rides are deeply intertwined with Lanzarote's history. For centuries, these sturdy creatures were essential for transportation and work on the island. Today, they offer visitors a chance to channel the past while exploring the island's natural beauty. Imagine swaying gently atop a camel as you traverse trails connecting charming villages, pristine beaches, and awe-inspiring volcanoes. Lanzarote's diverse flora, fauna, and geological wonders will be your companions along the way. Companies like Camel Safari Park, Lanzarote Camel Ride, and Lanzarote Experience Tours are ready to help you plan an unforgettable camel adventure. Here are a few of Lanzarote's prime locations for camel rides:

- Timanfaya National Park: This park is undeniably Lanzarote's star attraction, a place where the raw power of volcanic forces is laid bare. Encompassing 51 square kilometers, it is Spain's only entirely geological national park. Lava fields in every direction, craters, calderas, even geysers – it's a landscape like no other. A visitor center offers information about the park, and there's even a restaurant where the chefs harness the volcano's heat for cooking! Choose from various ways to explore Timanfaya, including a guided bus tour, the Tremensana Trail for those who prefer to explore on foot, or a traditional camel ride.

- La Geria: Lanzarote's distinctive wine region covers an impressive 52 square kilometers. The ingenuity of the island's inhabitants is showcased in the unique way grapes are cultivated here. Individual vines are planted in holes dug directly into the volcanic soil, then covered with volcanic sand called picón. This layer is vital, helping vines retain moisture and providing protection from the elements. Stone walls known as "zocos" provide additional shelter. The grapes grown here, primarily the malvasia variety, produce high-quality wines. Camel rides through La Geria allow you to experience this special landscape while learning about the island's winemaking history and its connection to camels.

- La Graciosa: This tiny gem, the smallest in the Canary Islands, is also part of the protected Chinijo Archipelago Natural Park. With no paved roads and only bikes and jeeps for transportation, its 29 square kilometers are a haven of tranquility. Gentle hills, cliffs, and flat, sandy terrain make it perfect for exploring on camelback. La Graciosa boasts charming villages, pristine beaches, and picture-perfect views. Visit the island's museum for a glimpse into its past, including its ties to camels.

Jeep Safaris

For those who prefer a bit more speed and the ability to cover even more ground, jeep safaris are another excellent way to discover Lanzarote's wild beauty. Their versatility means you can reach places inaccessible to many other vehicles. Imagine exploring hidden coves, traversing volcanic landscapes and taking in panoramic vistas few visitors get to see. There's something undeniably exhilarating about bouncing along dirt roads surrounded by dramatic scenery. Many tour companies offer guided jeep safaris around the island, providing everything you'll need for a day of safe and adventurous exploration.

- Los Ajaches Natural Monument: Discover this awe-inspiring volcanic formation that dominates Lanzarote's southern region. The roughly 15-million-year-old landscape encompasses an incredible variety of terrain: hills, valleys, soaring cliffs, and even beaches. The diverse conditions have allowed a unique ecosystem to flourish, so keep your eyes peeled for native lizards, rabbits, birds, and fascinating plant species. Imagine bouncing along dirt tracks in your jeep, taking in breathtaking coastal views, and exploring some of the area's most iconic beaches. Playa de Papagayo, Playa de las Mujeres, Playa del Pozo, and Playa de la Cera are just a few of many potential stops on your jeep adventure.

- Mirador del Río: Prepare for jaw-dropping vistas from this viewpoint perched on Lanzarote's north coast. Gaze out over the Chinijo Archipelago and the Risco de Famara – a towering 500-meter cliff plunging dramatically into the Atlantic. Like many of Lanzarote's attractions, the Mirador del Río bears the distinctive touch of César Manrique. This former military battery was ingeniously transformed into a stunning viewpoint in the early 1970s. Using local volcanic rock, native plants, and integrating the structure seamlessly with its surroundings, Manrique created a harmonious space that celebrates its stunning natural setting. Your jeep safari can take you along a mix of paved roads and dirt tracks, delivering you to the Mirador del Río. From this vantage point, soak in panoramic views and perhaps explore some nearby attractions like the Cueva de los Verdes, Jameos del Agua, or Jardín de Cactus.

- Caldera Blanca: Embark on a combination jeep safari and hiking adventure that takes you to the rim of Caldera Blanca, one of Lanzarote's most impressive volcanic craters. This immense crater, spanning 1.2 kilometers across with a depth of 200 meters, is the product of eruptions in 1730 and now lies within Timanfaya National Park. Your jeep can deliver you to the trailhead, conveniently located near the village of Mancha Blanca. From there, follow the well-marked path winding through lava fields and past smaller volcanic cones. Expect some steep sections and loose rocks, but most reasonably fit hikers will find the challenge manageable. The reward at the crater's rim is well worth the effort – sweeping views of nearby volcanoes, the sparkling ocean beyond, and even the island of La Graciosa.

Cultural Experiences

Museums and Art Galleries

César Manrique Foundation

This is undeniably one of the most significant museums in Lanzarote, and a must-visit for anyone interested in the life and works of César Manrique. This brilliant artist and architect left an indelible mark on Lanzarote, and the museum offers a unique opportunity to understand his vision. His former home and studio, located within the village of Tahíche, now function as the museum. Manrique masterfully integrated his creation into the surrounding lava field, blurring the lines between art, architecture, and the natural world. The building has two distinct sections. The upper level reflects traditional Canarian architectural styles and houses artwork by Manrique and other notable artists. The lower portion is perhaps the most fascinating – a series of rooms and interconnected spaces built into five volcanic bubbles. A garden, pool, fountain, and windmill complete the picture, creating a harmonious space respectful of the island's culture and environment. In addition to Manrique's paintings, drawings, ceramics, and murals, the museum also displays his personal items, offering glimpses into his life beyond his art. Guided tours, concerts, and exhibitions focused on his legacy are frequently hosted by the museum.

Lagomar Museum

If you appreciate the quirky and unexpected, a visit to the Lagomar Museum in the village of Nazaret is a must. This one-of-a-kind museum is housed within a former quarry and was once the home of iconic actor Omar Sharif. He reportedly fell head over heels for the property while filming in Lanzarote during the 1970s. Using volcanic rocks, local plants, and wood, the sprawling complex boasts a labyrinthine layout. Explore multiple levels, terraces, and paths – all designed to create a sense of discovery. A restored windmill provides a striking focal point, and a lake provides a beautiful juxtaposition with the rock and vegetation. Sculptures, paintings, and thoughtfully placed lighting add to the artistic ambiance. Sharif fans will enjoy seeing movie memorabilia like posters, photos, and costumes, as well as some of his personal belongings. Take a break in the cafeteria to soak up the remarkable setting, or browse for a memento in the souvenir shop.

For lovers of literature, the Casa José Saramago is a fascinating glimpse into the world of a Nobel Prize-winning author. Saramago made the village of Tías his home from 1993 until his death in 2010, and the museum is housed in his former residence. This simple, welcoming home is surrounded by a garden and a wall, offering a sense of the peace and tranquility he may have found here. The museum's mission is to preserve the home as Saramago knew it, complete with his own possessions – his furniture, paintings, and other objects. But the heart of the space is undoubtedly his impressive personal library, containing over 15,000 books spanning a broad spectrum of languages and genres. The study where he penned acclaimed works like "Blindness," "The Cave," and "The Double" remains as he left it. To enhance your visit, consider utilizing the museum's audio guide or taking a guided tour. These provide additional context and detail about Saramago's life and career and highlight his connection with the island of Lanzarote and its people. Readings, workshops, and conferences focused on promoting both the literary and human ideals that Saramago embodied are frequently hosted by the museum.

Historical Sites and Archaeological Sites
Castillo de San Gabriel

Step back in time to the 16th century by visiting this prominent historical landmark. The Castillo de San Gabriel was constructed to protect the island from relentless pirate attacks. This fortress occupies a small island linked to the city of Arrecife by a causeway and bridge. The castle's rectangular structure boasts four bastions, a moat, and a drawbridge – all designed with defense in mind. Within the castle, a museum houses informative exhibits detailing Lanzarote's rich history and culture. Examine weaponry, maps, period clothing, and historical documents. Perhaps the best part of a visit is the panoramic view the castle affords, encompassing both the city and the sparkling sea beyond.

Iron Man of Lanzarote

This striking statue located on the beach of Puerto del Carmen honors the 20th anniversary of the island's Ironman Triathlon. Standing 2.5 meters high, this 600-kilogram iron figure is a testament to the spirit of this grueling sporting event. The Ironman Triathlon, one of the most prestigious and challenging in the world, consists of a 3.8-kilometer swim, a 180-kilometer bike ride, and a 42.2-kilometer run. The Iron Man statue celebrates the connection between the athletes and Lanzarote and symbolizes the values inherent to the competition – endurance, perseverance, and unwavering solidarity. Located on Puerto del Carmen's promenade near the Hotel Los Fariones, it's a popular photo spot for locals and visitors alike. A plaque at the base lists the Ironman Lanzarote winners from 1992 to 2010.

La Molina – Gofio

For a taste of authentic Lanzarote, visit this traditional windmill once dedicated to the production of gofio. Found in the village of San Bartolomé, this windmill dates from the 18th century. Gofio, a cornerstone of traditional

Canarian cuisine, is made from roasted grains like wheat, barley, or corn. The windmill's distinctive shape features a conical roof and four wooden blades designed to rotate with the wind. An on-site museum houses original equipment and tools used to produce gofio and offers insights into the history behind this ancient food. Guided tours offer a unique chance to see the windmill at work and sample different gofio flavors and recipes.

Canarian Cuisine and Gastronomy
Typical Dishes

- Papas arrugadas con mojo: This dish is synonymous with the Canary Islands, and a mainstay of Lanzarote's restaurants. Small potatoes are cooked unpeeled in heavily salted water until the skins wrinkle as the water evaporates. These are served with mojo, a flavorful sauce whose most basic ingredients include garlic, oil, vinegar, salt, and spices. Mojo comes in two main varieties. Mojo rojo (or picón) is the spicy version, getting its red hue and fiery kick from paprika and chili peppers. Mojo verde tends to be milder, relying on parsley and cilantro for its distinctive flavors. Both papas arrugadas and mojo are the perfect accompaniment to fish, meat, or cheese.

- Sancocho: This hearty stew typically features salted fish like cherne (wreckfish) or corvina (croaker). The fish is boiled alongside potatoes, sweet potatoes, and an ingredient deeply rooted in the region's history – gofio. This roasted cereal flour is exceptionally high in nutrients and has been a staple food since the time of the Guanches, the Canary Islands' original inhabitants. Versatile gofio can be mixed with various liquids to create a dough or beverage. Sancocho is a dish traditionally enjoyed during Easter or other special occasions and is accompanied by mojo and salad.
- Ropa vieja: The name of this satisfying dish translates to "old clothes," a reference to how the shredded meat resembles torn rags. Ropa vieja can be made with chicken, beef, or pork and is simmered with chickpeas, potatoes, tomatoes, onions, garlic, and a mix of spices. While its roots lie in mainland Spain, the dish has been skillfully adapted to highlight Canarian ingredients. Commonly found on Lanzarote menus, ropa vieja is typically served with bread, rice, or gofio.

Typical Desserts

- Bienmesabe: Prepare your tastebuds for this sweet, creamy delight! The name translates to "it tastes good to me," and it's an accurate description. Ground almonds, sugar, eggs, lemon zest, and cinnamon are the stars of this dessert. Bienmesabe's origins lie in Arabic cuisine, though the Canarians have embraced it as their own. Usually served cold in small portions, it may be accompanied by ice cream, whipped cream, or a drizzle of honey.
- Frangollo: This simple yet comforting dessert relies on milk, corn flour, sugar, butter, eggs, raisins, almonds, lemon zest, and cinnamon. It boasts a thick, velvety texture and a sweet, aromatic flavor profile. Frangollo's ease of preparation means you'll find it in homes and restaurants alike. Depending on the season, it may be enjoyed hot or cold. Look for it served in bowls or cups, often with an extra sprinkle of cinnamon or sugar on top.

Quesillo: A Creamy, Custard-like Treat

This smooth, moist dessert is made with eggs, condensed milk, evaporated milk, sugar, and vanilla extract. It shares some similarities with flan or custard but tends to possess a denser, firmer texture. Cooking in a water bath is key to achieving quesillo's signature texture. After chilling, the dessert is usually unmolded and drizzled with caramel sauce. Whipped cream or fruit sometimes serve as accompaniments. Quesillo is a favorite in Lanzarote, readily available in bakeries and supermarkets. It's typically served in slices or wedges as a snack or satisfying end to a meal.

Typical Cheeses and Wines

- Queso de Lanzarote: Goat's milk is the foundation for this cheese, thanks to the island's abundant supply of high-quality milk. The cheese can range from white to yellowish and may have a soft or semi-hard texture. Mild to robust flavor variations are achieved through differences in the ripening process and type of rennet used. Queso de Lanzarote can be fresh, cured, or even smoked and comes in various shapes and sizes. Protected Designation of Origin status ensures its authenticity and quality. Locals enjoy it in many ways: as an appetizer alongside bread, mojo, or honey or incorporated into salads, soups, or stews.

- Malvasía de Lanzarote: The malvasía grape, the most widely grown grape varietal on Lanzarote, is the star of this wine. Look for a pale yellow to golden color and a bouquet that is both fruity and floral. You'll find dry and sweet versions to suit your preference. Malvasía de Lanzarote can be young, aged, or even sparkling and showcases a range of alcohol levels. Like the cheese, it boasts Protected Designation of Origin status. This wine pairs beautifully with an appetizer of cheese, fish, or seafood. It's also a lovely complement to desserts like pastries, fruits, or chocolate.

Traditional Festivals and Events

- Carnival: This island-wide celebration is one of Lanzarote's most well-attended, drawing massive crowds to watch parades bursting with elaborate floats, colorful costumes, lively music, and joyous dancing. The festivities usually occur in February or March, with the exact timing determined by the calendar year. While each town adds its own unique flair and theme, some of the most renowned Carnival celebrations can be found in

Arrecife, Puerto del Carmen, and Haria. Carnival comes to a close with the 'Burial of the Sardine.' This quirky ceremony involves burning a giant sardine effigy in a bonfire, representing the end of the celebrations and ushering in the Lenten season.

- Semana Santa (Holy Week): Lanzarote observes the week leading up to Easter with solemn religious processions commemorating the passion, death, and resurrection of Jesus Christ. Throughout Semana Santa, sacred icons and religious statues are carried through the streets of numerous villages and towns. Some of the most awe-inspiring processions can be witnessed in Teguise, Yaiza, and San Bartolomé. Semana Santa is also a time to indulge in the local cuisine, especially the fish dishes and torrijas – a sweet bread pudding soaked in milk, eggs, and honey.
- Día de la Cruz (Day of the Cross): May 3rd is the date of this celebration honoring the cross as a symbol of faith and protection. Crosses throughout the island are adorned with intricate decorations of flowers, fruits, and other adornments. They're then displayed in public spaces like streets, squares, and churches. Some of the most elaborate and vibrant displays can be found in Haria, Teguise, and

Tinajo. Traditional folk music and dancing, games, and crafts are all part of the Día de la Cruz festivities.

- San Juan: Celebrating the summer solstice, San Juan unfolds on June 23rd and 24th. This is a night steeped in fire, magic, and a touch of superstition. Bonfires blaze brightly as people jump over the flames and make wishes. Water also plays a significant role, with some believing a swim in the sea or fountain will bestow health and happiness. Popular spots to experience all the San Juan revelry include Arrieta, Haria, and Teguise.

- Fiesta de Nuestra Señora de los Dolores (Our Lady of Sorrows): This festival honoring Lanzarote's patron saint takes place on September 15th. It pays tribute to the Virgin of the Volcanoes, who is believed to have interceded on the island's behalf during the volcanic eruptions of the 1730s. Pilgrims from every corner of Lanzarote and beyond, often clad in traditional costumes, journey on foot to the church in Mancha Blanca, where the image of the Virgin is revered. Offerings of fruits, vegetables, and even animals are presented. A craft fair, livestock show, and a festive folk festival round out the celebration.

- Festival of Volcanic Kitchens: This gastronomic event spotlights the culinary creativity and heritage of Lanzarote. Held in October, it gives local chefs, producers, and winemakers a platform to showcase their products and dishes through tastings, workshops, and demonstrations. Expect to find live music, art exhibitions, and cultural activities happening alongside the culinary focus. The Timanfaya National Park serves as the main venue for the festival, where chefs even harness the volcanic heat for cooking demonstrations!

Local Markets and Crafts

- Teguise Market: This market reigns supreme as the largest and most well-known on Lanzarote – perhaps even in the entire Canary Island chain! Each Sunday, from 9:00 to 14:00, the historic center of Teguise, the island's former capital, transforms into a bustling marketplace. Expect to find a vast array of items, including handmade souvenirs, pottery, jewelry, leather goods, clothing, food, and much more. Live music and street performers enhance the festive ambiance. For a dose of Lanzarote history, combine your market visit with a trip to the nearby Castillo de Santa Bárbara, a 16th-century fortress with a pirate museum.

- Haria Market: If you're looking for an authentic, charming market experience, Haria Market should be on your list. Every Saturday from 10:00 to 14:30, the Plaza León y Castillo within this picturesque village, surrounded by palm trees, comes alive with the market. Local products abound – cheese, wine, honey, a bounty of fresh fruits and vegetables, and delightful pastries. You'll also discover handicrafts like baskets, embroidery, ceramics, and woodwork. Be sure to soak up the traditional Lanzarote culture showcased through folk music, dancing, and craft demonstrations.

- Marina Rubicon Market: For a market with a modern, stylish feel, head to the Marina Rubicon Market in Playa Blanca, a popular resort town. Open every Wednesday and Saturday from 10:00 to 14:00, this market is situated within the Puerto Deportivo Marina Rubicon. Clothing, accessories, jewelry, perfumes, cosmetics, and souvenirs are plentiful, and you're likely to find some local crafts and artwork as well. The picturesque marina setting offers stunning views of boats, the sparkling sea, and the neighboring islands of Fuerteventura and Lobos.

- Uga Market: Discover this small and welcoming market in the village of Uga, located near Timanfaya National Park. Open Saturdays and Sundays from 9:00 to 14:00, this is the place to go for fresh, organic produce like cheese, meat, eggs, bread, jams, and sauces. Pottery, paintings, and sculptures represent some of the handicrafts you may find. The market also provides an excellent opportunity to see Lanzarote's famous camels, often used for tours of the nearby volcanic park.
- Mancha Blanca Market: This rural market with a focus on eco-friendly products takes place in the village where the church of Nuestra Señora de los Dolores (patron saint of Lanzarote) is located. Every Sunday from 9:00 to 14:00, locals and visitors browse stalls laden with local and organic products such as cheese, fish, pastries, herbs, and spices. Candles, soap, and jewelry are among the handcrafted goods, and there's even a dedicated section showcasing Lanzarote's culinary tradition of cooking with volcanic heat.

- Costa Teguise Craft Market: This unique market offers a blend of art, local craftsmanship, and a lively atmosphere. Every Friday from 18:00 to 22:00, it takes place in the Plaza Pueblo Marinero within the bustling resort town of Costa Teguise. Expect to find one-of-a-kind creations like paintings, sculptures, jewelry, leather goods, and textiles, all made by talented local artisans. Live music, performances, and exhibitions add to the cultural and bohemian vibe.

Practical Information

Accommodation Options

Hotels

The Luxury Retreat: La Isla y el Mar, Hotel Boutique

If you crave the finer things in life, La Isla y el Mar Hotel Boutique in Puerto del Carmen will be your haven. This 5-star gem delivers impeccable service, elegant design, and breathtaking views. Unwind alongside their stunning outdoor pools, pamper yourself with a relaxing treatment at the spa, or work up a sweat at their fitness center. After a satisfying day, dine at their exquisite restaurant offering delightful cuisine that will tantalize your tastebuds.

Retire to your luxurious, air-conditioned suite complete with a private balcony or terrace – the perfect spot to take in the mesmerizing views. Your suite comes equipped with a minibar, coffee machine, and flat-screen TV, ensuring all your needs for a comfortable stay are met. With bike rental, car hire, and airport shuttle services at your fingertips, explore the treasures of Lanzarote with ease.

The Rural Escape: Caserío de Mozaga

For a true taste of Lanzarote's unique charm, tranquility, and authenticity, Caserío de Mozaga is an exceptional choice. Situated in the quaint village of Mozaga, this 3-star hotel sits at the heart of the island, a stone's throw away from the otherworldly Timanfaya National Park and the picturesque La Geria wine region. Housed within a beautifully restored 18th-century farmhouse, this hotel exudes history and character.

Each room is imbued with rustic charm; think exposed wooden beams, warm stone walls, and carefully chosen antique furnishings. After a day of exploration, let the hotel's restaurant entice you with delicious, traditional Canarian flavors. Then unwind with a drink at the bar, lose yourself in a captivating book from the library, or simply soak in the serene ambiance on the charming terrace.

Casa de las Flores - Hotel Boutique Lanzarote

Located in the historic town of Teguise, Casa de las Flores - Hotel Boutique Lanzarote, is a haven for art and culture enthusiasts. This 4-star boutique hotel bursts with personality. A profusion of flowers, vibrant paintings, intriguing sculptures, and a myriad of other artistic flourishes adorn the space, creating a unique and captivating atmosphere.

Step into your stylish, modern room where a private balcony awaits, perfect for sipping your morning coffee. A minibar, coffee machine, and smart TV ensure a comfortable and connected stay. After soaking up the hotel's vibrant ambiance, indulge in a delicious meal at the restaurant or unwind with a beverage at the bar. Revel in the peaceful atmosphere as you wander through the picturesque garden and relax on the inviting terrace.

Hotel Rural Finca de La Florida
For a truly one-of-a-kind experience, Hotel Rural Finca de La Florida near San Bartolomé offers a memorable stay steeped in history and surrounded by natural beauty. Nestled right near the iconic César Manrique Foundation and the moving Campesino Monument, this 3-star hotel occupies a beautifully converted former winery. The traditional Canarian architecture, with its pristine white

walls and vibrant green windows, immediately transports you to another era.

Classic-style rooms with private balconies, minibars, and satellite TVs provide a comfortable respite after days filled with adventure. When you're not out in the sun, take a refreshing dip in the hotel's pool, challenge yourself in the fitness center, or unwind in the restorative sauna. Mini-golf and a tempting restaurant add to the list of enjoyable amenities. And if you're feeling adventurous, the hotel offers a range of activities like hiking, biking, and even horseback riding – the perfect way to explore the island's stunning landscapes.

Resorts

Princesa Yaiza Suite Hotel Resort

Experience the ultimate in island relaxation within the luxurious 5-star confines of the Princesa Yaiza Suite Hotel Resort. Nestled within the lively resort town of Playa Blanca, renowned for its captivating beaches and vibrant marina, this resort offers a true sanctuary. Pamper yourself in their spacious and elegantly designed suites – some even boast breathtaking sea views and the added indulgence of a private jacuzzi.

With a staggering eight outdoor pools at your disposal, the resort provides ample opportunity to bask in the Lanzarote sun. Unwind with a pampering treatment at the spa, invigorate your body at the fitness center, and let your little ones have the time of their lives at the kids' club. Culinary adventures await at the resort's delectable selection of restaurants and bars. Discover the magic of the nearby Papagayo beaches, immerse yourself in the natural wonders of the Timanfaya National Park, and explore the charms of the Marina Rubicon – all within easy reach.

H10 Rubicon Palace
Nestled near Playa Blanca's iconic lighthouse and the pristine Flamingo beach, the 4-star H10 Rubicon Palace exudes modern style. White buildings adorned with colorful accents provide a striking and contemporary backdrop for your Lanzarote getaway. Retreat to bright

and airy guest rooms, many offering private balconies or terraces for soaking in the island atmosphere.

When you're not exploring, take advantage of the resort's six sparkling outdoor pools, rejuvenate at the luxurious spa, stay in shape at the well-equipped gym, or let loose with the lively entertainment provided by the dedicated mini club. With a rich selection of dining options at your fingertips, your tastebuds are sure to be tantalized. Plus, the proximity to the enchanting Papagayo beaches, the awe-inspiring Timanfaya National Park, and the lively Marina Rubicon promise adventures aplenty.

Seaside Los Jameos Playa
The 4-star Seaside Los Jameos Playa sits within the vibrant town of Puerto del Carmen, a true Lanzarote hotspot known for its expansive beaches and bustling nightlife. This resort effortlessly blends traditional Canarian architecture, with its whitewashed walls and vibrant green windows, with modern amenities for a truly satisfying vacation.

Rest comfortably in spacious, inviting rooms – some offering balconies with direct sea views for an extra dose of tranquility. Make a splash in one of the four outdoor pools, indulge in soothing spa treatments, get competitive on the tennis court, or enjoy a leisurely round of mini-golf. Evenings promise culinary delights at the resort's tempting buffet restaurant. Explore the captivating Rancho Texas Lanzarote Park, immerse yourself in the artistic legacy of César Manrique at his Foundation, or practice your swing at the Lanzarote Golf Resort – all conveniently located nearby.

Barceló Teguise Beach

Discover a contemporary oasis in Costa Teguise, where the 4-star Barceló Teguise Beach awaits. Known for its sandy beaches and ideal windsurfing conditions, this vibrant resort town provides the ideal backdrop for your Lanzarote escape. Immerse yourself in the sleek and minimalist design of this resort, accented with soothing shades of white and blue.

Contemporary rooms offer comfortable accommodations – upgrade to those with sea views and private jacuzzis for an extra touch of indulgence. Two welcoming outdoor pools provide ample opportunities for soaking up the sun. Rejuvenate with a visit to the resort's spa, work up a sweat at the fitness center, and keep your tastebuds happy with the tempting on-site restaurant. The Aquapark Costa Teguise, the enchanting Cactus Garden, and the historic Castillo de Santa Bárbara offer nearby adventures.

Villas
Villa Alba
If your dream island getaway includes nothing short of the finest accommodations, Villa Alba promises to deliver. This 5-star villa sits within the prestigious Puerto Calero, known for its sophisticated marina brimming with luxurious yachts, exquisite restaurants, and chic shops. Indulge in the villa's four opulent bedrooms and four impeccably appointed bathrooms, providing ample space for relaxation and privacy. You'll find a fully equipped kitchen ready to inspire culinary adventures, a spacious

living room for unwinding, and a dining room perfect for lingering over delicious meals.

Step outside and take full advantage of your private villa paradise. Enjoy a refreshing dip in the heated pool, slip into the bubbling jacuzzi, or unwind in the restorative sauna. Let the aromas of sizzling meals dance in the air as you utilize the barbecue, then dine al fresco as you take in breathtaking views. Your vantage point from the rooftop terrace offers unforgettable panoramas showcasing the sea, majestic mountains, and the bustling marina below.

Villa El Aljibe
For those seeking an escape steeped in authentic charm and peaceful seclusion, Villa El Aljibe delivers a true Canarian experience. Nestled within the traditional village of Tinajo, at the very heart of the island, this 4-star villa grants you access to both the otherworldly landscapes of the Timanfaya National Park and the adrenaline-fueled waves of the La Santa surf spot.

History comes to life in this impeccably restored 18th-century farmhouse – original wooden beams, warm stone walls, and an ancient cistern are testament to its rich past. Two cozy bedrooms and two bathrooms offer comfortable respite, while the kitchen, living room, and dining room provide a welcoming space to gather. Outside, your own private pool awaits, surrounded by a flourishing garden and a quaint patio perfect for savoring the tranquil atmosphere.

Villa Lanzarote Natura
Located in the residential area of Tahiche, near the iconic César Manrique Foundation and the captivating Cactus Garden, Villa Lanzarote Natura exudes a unique and artistic charm. Within this 4-star villa, discover vibrant contemporary art, fascinating sculptures, and eye-catching murals adorning the space, creating an atmosphere that is both inspiring and stylish.

Ideal for families or groups of friends, the villa offers three bedrooms and two bathrooms, along with ample shared living spaces like the kitchen, living room, and dining room. Embrace long, sunny days in your private oasis, complete with a heated pool, jacuzzi, barbecue, and a relaxing terrace – perfect for soaking up the Lanzarote sun or enjoying a meal under the stars.

Villa Volcan

Escape to the rural haven of La Asomada, where Villa Volcan offers a unique stay steeped in history and surrounded by breathtaking natural beauty. Here, stunning views of the sea, majestic mountains, and picturesque vineyards are your constant companions. This 3-star villa is built directly into a volcanic cave, lending a rustic and undeniably cozy charm to your stay. Wooden furnishings, stone floors, and a cozy fireplace enhance the warm ambiance.

The villa houses two bedrooms and a bathroom, along with a kitchen, living room, and dining area – all the comforts of home in this spectacular setting. Outside, your senses will be delighted. Take a refreshing dip in the private pool, relax in the garden, or simply embrace the extraordinary views and volcanic surroundings from your private balcony.

Apartments

Apartamentos Fariones

For those desiring an upscale experience in the bustling heart of Puerto del Carmen, Apartamentos Fariones provides the ideal blend of style and location. This 4-star apartment complex offers a refined atmosphere and convenient proximity to a wealth of restaurants, bars, and shops. Choose from well-appointed one or two-bedroom apartments, each boasting a private balcony or terrace where you can take in the ambiance. Inside, expect a fully equipped kitchen, a spacious living room, a comfortable bathroom, and all the modern amenities you desire like air conditioning, Wi-Fi, and a flat-screen TV.

The complex itself ensures your leisure time is well-spent. Soak up the sun on the sprawling terrace surrounding the outdoor pool, unwind in the lush garden, or seek friendly assistance at the 24-hour reception. And when you're ready to explore, the expansive sands of Playa Grande, the alluring Biosfera shopping center, and the exciting Rancho Texas Lanzarote Park are all within easy reach.

Finca Marisa

Escape to the quiet village of Tinajo and discover the traditional charms of Finca Marisa. This inviting 3-star apartment complex offers a peaceful respite close to the otherworldly Timanfaya National Park and the adrenaline-inducing waves of famed surf spot La Santa. Within your rustic-style apartment, find respite in one or two cozy bedrooms, whip up tasty meals in the kitchen, relax in the living room, and take in the authentic Lanzarote vibe from your private patio or terrace. The use of warm wood furnishings, traditional stone walls, and splashes of color create a welcoming atmosphere.

Relaxation awaits throughout the complex. Take a dip in the heated pool, luxuriate in the jacuzzi, unwind in the sauna, and savor a meal fresh off the barbecue. Evenings promise serene moments in the inviting lounge. For your adventures, explore the otherworldly El Jable desert, delve into the local culture at the La Vegueta market, and be inspired by the artistic legacy at the César Manrique Foundation – all conveniently located nearby.

Lanzarote Ocean View

Immerse yourself in the fishing village of Arrieta and experience the unique blend of modern style and artistic flair at Lanzarote Ocean View. This 4-star apartment complex sits along the island's north coast, granting you access to sandy beaches and tranquil natural pools. One and two-bedroom apartments are yours to choose from, each equipped with a private balcony or terrace, perfect for savoring the ocean vistas.

Inside, discover a contemporary aesthetic where soothing whites and blues are accented by original paintings and sculptures. A comfortable living room, well-appointed kitchen, and relaxing bathroom complete your home away from home. Venture out to enjoy the complex's rooftop terrace offering breathtaking views, find peace in the lush garden, or lose yourself in a good book from the inviting library. Lanzarote's iconic sites like the Jameos del Agua, the Cueva de los Verdes, and the Mirador del Río viewpoint are easily accessible for unforgettable adventures.

Casa Tomarén

Experience island living infused with history at Casa Tomarén. Situated in the rural heart of Lanzarote near the Campesino Monument and the picturesque La Geria wine region, this 3-star complex is housed within a restored 18th-century country house. Original architectural features like exposed wooden beams, warm stone floors, and even a traditional cistern add to the unique allure.

Within your one or two-bedroom apartment, a welcoming kitchen, cozy living area, relaxing bathroom, and a private patio or terrace await. Unwind by the outdoor pool, find your Zen in the yoga room, indulge in a soothing massage, and savor delectable meals at the on-site restaurant. When adventure calls, the complex offers a variety of activities like hiking, biking, and even horseback riding, allowing you to fully immerse yourself in Lanzarote's stunning natural landscapes.

To explore more and also book your accommodation, you can visit: www.tripadvisor.com

Dining and Eating Out

Casa Rafa Restaurante de Mar

Immerse yourself in the authentic flavors of the Canaries at Casa Rafa Restaurante de Mar. Nestled in the charming fishing village of El Golfo, known for its striking black sand beach and vibrant green lagoon, this restaurant is a haven for seafood lovers. Step into a cozy atmosphere, where rustic wooden tables and warm stone walls set a welcoming ambiance while offering glimpses of the sea beyond.

Casa Rafa prides itself on using fresh, locally sourced ingredients and traditional recipes. Savor the flavors of succulent fish, tender prawns, expertly cooked octopus, and plump mussels. Each dish is prepared with care, showcasing the island's culinary heritage – whether grilled to perfection, delicately fried, or bathed in a flavorful sauce. Accompany your feast with classic Canarian side dishes like papas arrugadas (wrinkled potatoes) drizzled in the distinctive mojo sauce or the nutty richness of gofio (toasted corn flour).

La Cocina de Colacho

Discover a dining experience that tantalizes both your palate and your creative spirit at La Cocina de Colacho. Located in the vibrant resort town of Playa Blanca, renowned for its pristine beaches and lively marina, this stylish restaurant is the brainchild of renowned chef Joaquín Espejo, affectionately known as Colacho.

Embark on a culinary adventure where traditional ingredients meet cutting-edge techniques. Chef Colacho's creations are both a feast for the eyes and a delight for the tastebuds – each dish bursting with flavor and unexpected combinations. As you dine, be captivated by the works of local artists adorning the walls. Paintings, sculptures, and murals infuse the space with vibrant colors and textures, creating a truly unique ambiance.

Restaurante Mirador de Los Valles

Escape to the picturesque village of Los Valles in northern Lanzarote for a dining experience that celebrates nature's bounty at Restaurante Mirador de Los Valles. Nestled in a landscape known for the Mirador del Río viewpoint and the captivating Cueva de los Verdes, this restaurant is an extension of a charming rural hotel. Prepare to be delighted by a menu that changes with the seasons, reflecting the freshest local ingredients.

Expect cheeses, wines, honey, an abundance of fruits and vegetables, and tender meats – all sourced with care from the surrounding region. Vegetarian, vegan, and gluten-free options are thoughtfully crafted, ensuring everyone can revel in the fresh, wholesome flavors. Dine within a warm and inviting atmosphere defined by wooden furnishings, stone floors, and breathtaking panoramas of the valley stretching out to the sea.

Restaurante El Diablo

For a truly unforgettable dining experience, venture into the heart of Timanfaya National Park – a natural marvel showcasing Lanzarote's dramatic volcanic landscapes. Discover Restaurante El Diablo, a unique eatery built directly atop a volcanic vent. Here, the relentless heat emanating from the earth itself is harnessed to create extraordinary dishes.

Watch as skilled chefs work their magic over a massive grill, cooking succulent meats, delicate fish, and fresh vegetables directly over the volcanic heat. Complement your meal with a selection from the buffet offering salads, flavorful soups, and delectable desserts. The restaurant's circular design and floor-to-ceiling windows grant mesmerizing views of the otherworldly volcanic formations surrounding you.

Transportation
Bus
For budget-friendly travel across Lanzarote's main towns, resorts, and popular attractions, the island's public bus system is a convenient choice. Expect to travel in modern buses with comfortable seats and air-conditioning, making

even longer journeys pleasant. Single tickets or "bono cards" offer a discount on multiple journeys, keeping your transportation costs down. Intercity Bus Lanzarote operates the system, and you can easily find routes, schedules, and pricing information directly on their website.

It's important to note that service to some of the island's more remote areas or unique landmarks might be infrequent or nonexistent. Additionally, depending on the time of year and traffic conditions, schedules may not always be strictly adhered to.

Taxi

When speed and convenience are key, Lanzarote's taxi network is readily available across the entire island. Easily identify official taxis by their white color and distinctive "taxi" signage displayed on the roof. Hail one directly on the street, arrange a pickup by phone, or head to taxi ranks often located near the airport, bus stations, shopping areas, and popular tourist spots.

Taxi fares are government-regulated and metered, tending to be more affordable than in areas like Northern Europe. Check approximate fares on the Lanzarote Taxi website. Taxis are a fantastic option for shorter distances, avoiding the need to find parking, or even for a safe ride home after a night out Just remember, depending on the time of day, your destination, and overall demand, availability and cost can fluctuate.

Car Rental

If you desire the utmost freedom to fully explore Lanzarote at your leisure, renting a vehicle might be the perfect fit. Choose from a broad selection of cars – from compact and economical to luxurious and spacious vans – offered by established companies like Cicar, Avis, and Europcar. Book your rental online, by phone, or directly at the airport. Rental prices are competitive and generally include insurance, taxes, and unlimited mileage. Check comparison sites like Lanzarote Car Hire to compare rates and rental terms across different companies.

To rent a car, you will need a valid driver's license, a credit card, and must meet the specified minimum age (this varies between companies and vehicle types, but generally falls between 21 and 23 years old).

Ferry

For those wanting to extend their Lanzarote adventure to other nearby islands, a relaxing ferry ride might be the perfect way to travel. Connect to Fuerteventura, Gran Canaria, or the charming La Graciosa via comfortable ferries offering amenities like bars, restaurants, shops, and even entertainment onboard. Several companies like Fred Olsen, Naviera Armas, and Lineas Romero operate these routes. Purchase your tickets online, by phone, or directly at the port.

Ferry prices vary depending on your route, season of travel, and whether you're traveling as a passenger or with a vehicle. You can find detailed scheduling and pricing information on the Lanzarote Ferry website. Keep in mind, rough seas or high demand can sometimes influence ferry availability and travel times.

Bike

For the physically fit and adventurous traveler, renting a bike is a fantastic way to experience Lanzarote's beauty while getting some great exercise. Choose from a variety of options like mountain bikes, road bikes, tandem bikes, and even electric bikes to suit your needs and preferences. Companies like Papagayo Bike, ProAction BH, and Lanzarote Bike offer rentals with convenient online booking or you can arrange everything by phone or in person. Expect reasonable prices that include helmets, locks, and even maps to help you navigate.

While exploring by bike is a rewarding and eco-friendly way to see the island, always keep safety in mind. Be physically prepared for the challenge, remain mindful of traffic, and show respect for the island's natural environment.

Safety Tips and Emergency Contacts

Safety Tips

- **Protecting Yourself from Petty Crime:** Lanzarote is generally a safe destination for travelers, but it's essential to be mindful of opportunistic crimes like pickpocketing and scams, especially in popular tourist spots. Remain vigilant with your belongings, particularly in crowded places like markets, busy beaches, and when traveling on buses. Keep valuables secured close to your body and out of sight. Be cautious of people approaching you with clipboards, petitions, or seemingly unbelievable offers. These could be tactics to distract you and steal your possessions, or to solicit money in exchange for worthless items. If you encounter these situations, a firm "no thank you" and confidently walking away is your best course of action.

- **Ensuring Your Accommodation is Safe and Secure:** When selecting a villa or apartment, prioritize choosing one that has a secure feel and offers a safe for storing your important documents, cash, and electronics. Always practice good security habits – lock doors and windows upon leaving and before going to bed. Avoid leaving valuables in plain sight to deter opportunistic theft. Should any major problems or concerns arise with your accommodation, don't hesitate to contact your rental company or property owner promptly for assistance.

- **Responsible Driving & Cycling:** If exploring Lanzarote by car or bike, it's paramount that you adhere to all traffic laws and regulations, showing respect to other drivers, cyclists, and pedestrians. Always remember to wear your seatbelt when in a car and a helmet when cycling. Drinking and driving is never acceptable and carries serious consequences. Before starting your journey, take a few minutes to inspect your vehicle or rental bike, ensuring it is in good working condition and that you have all required insurance documentation. In the unfortunate event of an accident or breakdown, contact emergency services for immediate assistance or reach out to your rental company for support.

- **Protection from the Sun & Heat:** Lanzarote boasts a warm and sunny climate – perfect for enjoying those beautiful beaches! But remember to take precautions against risks like sunburn, dehydration, and even heatstroke. Staying hydrated is key, so carry water and drink plenty throughout the day, especially if enjoying the outdoors. Limit your consumption of alcohol and caffeinated beverages, as these can accelerate dehydration. Apply sunscreen liberally (even on cloudy days!) and reapply frequently. Protect your eyes with sunglasses and consider a wide-brimmed hat for additional shade. During the hottest part of the day, seek respite from the direct sun. Be cautious when swimming – never swim alone or in unfamiliar areas and always pay close attention to beach flags and posted signs.

- **Respecting Lanzarote's Volcanic Landscape:** The stunning volcanic landscapes are a major draw for visitors, but it's important to remain aware of their inherent potential for seismic activity. While major eruptions haven't occurred recently, the island remains active. Stay informed about the possibility of earthquakes, landslides, or changes in volcanic activity. In case of any emergency, always follow the guidance and instructions provided by local authorities and news outlets. Additionally, show respect for this unique and delicate environment – avoid disturbing, damaging, or removing any rocks, plants, or wildlife from protected volcanic areas.

Emergency Contacts

- **Universal Emergency Number:** If any situation arises requiring urgent assistance from the police, fire department, or medical services, dial 112. This is the local emergency number for Lanzarote.
- **Hospital Insular de Lanzarote:** For non-emergency medical situations requiring hospitalization or specialized care, the Hospital Insular de Lanzarote is the island's main public hospital. Their phone number is +34 928 59 50 00 and they are located at Juan de Quesada, s/n, 35500, Arrecife. The hospital has a dedicated emergency department, pharmacy, and other specialized units. Remember to bring your European Health Insurance Card (EHIC) and passport to access public healthcare.

Insider's Guide

Off the Beaten Path Attractions

El Golfo

Situated on Lanzarote's western coast, the quaint fishing village of El Golfo offers a visual feast unlike any other. Its star attraction is the Charco de Los Clicos, a vivid green lagoon formed within a volcanic crater. The algae thriving within create a captivating color contrast against the backdrop of black volcanic sand and the azure sea. Nearby, the secluded Playa del Golfo, known for its black sand, invites you to unwind and take in dramatic views of cliffs and crashing waves. And to complete the experience, El Golfo is the ideal spot to indulge in the freshest seafood. Local restaurants specialize in expertly prepared fish, prawns, octopus, and mussels – cooked to perfection in various styles, from grilled to fried to flavorful sauces.

Las Grietas: Miniature Volcanic Canyons

For a unique geological wonder, venture to Las Grietas. These three cracks formed along the slopes of the 600-

meter-tall Montaña Blanca volcano resemble a scaled-down version of the canyons found in Arizona or Utah. While not particularly long in distance, the cracks are quite narrow, offering a sense of awe-inspiring enclosure as you admire the intricate lines carved into the rock. Las Grietas rewards visitors with incredible views of Puerto del Carmen and the vast ocean beyond.

Bajo de la Montaña

Travel to the island's heart and discover Bajo de la Montaña, a volcanic crater near the town of San Bartolomé. Measuring roughly 200 meters wide and 30 meters deep, the crater boasts a circular shape and surprisingly flat bottom. Bajo de la Montaña is open to the public, inviting you to walk directly inside and explore its fascinating features. Keep an eye out for lava tubes, vents, and a variety of unique rock formations. The crater also serves as a fantastic spot to observe the island's distinctive flora and fauna – lizards, birds, and cacti are commonly spotted here.

Playa del Pozo

For a true escape, set your sights on Playa del Pozo, tucked away on Lanzarote's northeast coast near the town of Orzola. This hidden gem requires a bit more effort to reach, involving a walk along a dirt road and a rocky path. But the reward is well worth it – pristine white sands and mesmerizing turquoise waters await. The tranquil atmosphere is perfect for snorkeling; the clear, calm water is teeming with colorful fish and diverse marine life. Playa del Pozo is the ideal choice for those seeking a tranquil beach experience away from the hustle and bustle.

Guided Walks for Deeper Exploration

Timanfaya National Park is a must-visit Lanzarote attraction, showcasing the island's awe-inspiring volcanic power. The park encompasses over 51 square kilometers, featuring more than 25 volcanoes, striking lava fields, geysers, and craters. While a bus tour provides a fantastic overview of highlights like the Montañas del Fuego, the Islote de Hilario, and the Echadero de Camellos, consider venturing off the typical path with a guided walk. These walks take you deeper into the park, exploring less-traveled and spectacular areas like the Caldera Blanca, the Volcán Nuevo del Fuego, and the Ruta de los Volcanes. Guided walks are complimentary, but advance booking is essential due to limited spots and high demand.

Hidden Gems and Secret Spots
Charco de San Ginés

Step into a scene of postcard-perfect beauty in the capital of Lanzarote at the Charco de San Ginés. This natural lagoon, embraced by traditional white houses, swaying palms, and colorful fishing boats creates a sense of tranquility and timeless charm. This lively waterfront area is also a hub of culture, dotted with bars, inviting restaurants, unique shops, and galleries showcasing local art. A stroll across the historic Puente de las Bolas bridge will lead you to the Castillo de San Gabriel, a 16th-century fortress transformed into a museum, offering a glimpse into the island's past.

Charco del Palo: A Haven for Naturists

For those seeking a truly liberating experience in harmony with nature, head to Charco del Palo – a naturist village nestled on Lanzarote's northeastern coast, not far from Mala. This secluded village offers the ultimate sense of peace and freedom, where you can shed your clothes and worries. A tranquil natural pool called El Muro invites you to swim and soak in the sun's rays, while hidden rocky coves and inviting beaches beckon. If you choose to stay awhile, the village offers accommodation options like apartments and bungalows and even has a restaurant and supermarket for your convenience.

Charco Verde: A Tranquil Emerald Lagoon

Discover another of Lanzarote's vibrant green lagoons, Charco Verde, along the western coast near the village of El Golfo. While smaller and perhaps less known than Charco de los Clicos, this lagoon offers a more intimate and serene atmosphere. Witness the vivid green hue, a result of the unique algae flourishing in the water, contrasting beautifully against the black volcanic sand and the azure blue sea. Charco Verde is also a haven for birdwatchers keen to spot species like vibrant flamingos, graceful herons, and snowy egrets.

El Puente de las Bolas: A Natural Masterpiece

Journey to Lanzarote's north coast near the town of Orzola to marvel at El Puente de las Bolas – a natural arch sculpted by the relentless forces of nature. The arch, composed of basalt rock, boasts a circular shape with a distinctive central hole, resembling a ball. Located in a wild and untamed landscape, waves crash dramatically against the cliffs here, and strong winds add an element of elemental power. From this vantage point, you'll also be treated to views of La Graciosa Island, a mere 2 kilometers away.

Los Hervideros: Where the Sea Creates Drama

Witness the spectacular dance between land and sea at Los Hervideros along the southwestern coast near Yaiza. This series of caves and blowholes has been relentlessly carved by the ocean. The name, meaning "the boiling pots," perfectly describes the effect created as water rushes in and out of the caves – a mesmerizing display of bubbles, splashes, and echoing sounds. This dynamic sight is even more awe-inspiring when the sea is rough and the tide high. Walk along designated paths and platforms for breathtaking views of the caves, coastline, and open sea.

Mirador de la Ermita de las Nieves

Ascend to Lanzarote's highest point, standing 608 meters above sea level, for breathtaking vistas from the Mirador de la Ermita de las Nieves viewpoint. Located next to a charming small chapel honoring the island's patron saint, the Virgin of the Snows, this viewpoint grants you sweeping panoramas of the entire island. Gaze out at the sea and neighboring islands including La Graciosa, Alegranza, Montaña Clara, and Roque del Oeste. As the day draws to a close, this viewpoint transforms into a prime spot to watch the vibrant colors of sunset paint the sky.

Telamon's Stranded Ship: An Eerie Maritime Relic

Off the coast of Arrecife near the port of Los Mármoles, discover a curious and haunting sight – the half-sunken wreck of Telamon. This cargo ship met its fate in 1981, running aground in a fierce storm. Abandoned and left to the elements, the ship's rusting form holds a certain eerie intrigue. While it's not recommended to attempt to board the decaying ship, you can capture unique photos of this unusual landmark from a safe distance on the shore.

Tips for Immersing Yourself

The Power of Language

While many Lanzarote residents working in tourism have some understanding of English, making an effort to learn a few key Spanish phrases demonstrates a genuine desire to connect with the local culture. Start with the basics – greetings, simple questions, numbers, and directions. Phrasebooks, dictionaries, and translation apps are invaluable learning tools. Don't be afraid to try, even if your pronunciation isn't perfect! Locals will appreciate your effort and often happily help you learn. Additionally, try to pick up a few words or phrases specific to the Canary Islands, like "guagua" (bus), "papas" (potatoes), or "mojo" (sauce).

Savor the Island Flavors: Eat Like a Local

Food is deeply intertwined with the cultural fabric of Lanzarote, and stepping outside typical tourist restaurants to savor authentic local cuisine offers a delicious journey of discovery. Seek out establishments frequented by locals and indulge in traditional dishes like "sancocho" (fish stew), "ropa vieja" (a hearty meat and chickpea stew), or "conejo al salmorejo" (rabbit braised in a garlicky sauce). For a lively experience, visit bustling markets like the Teguise Market or the Uga Market. Here you'll find an abundance of locally sourced treasures – cheeses, wines, honey, fresh fruits and vegetables, and tempting pastries. To take your culinary adventure even further, consider joining a cooking class or dedicated food tour, where you'll learn firsthand about the island's unique ingredients and cooking traditions.

Celebrate with the Community

Lanzarote boasts a rich and vibrant cultural calendar filled with events and festivals that showcase the island's music, art, and traditions. Investigate schedules for local concerts, perhaps featuring traditional Canarian music, or lively comedy shows and even classical theatre performances. If your travels coincide with one of the island's major festivals, don't miss the opportunity to immerse yourself in the celebration! Experience the colorful costumes, lively parades, traditional dances, and even fireworks during events like Carnival, the Fiesta de San Juan, or the Fiesta de Nuestra Señora de los Dolores.

Stay Among the Locals

Choose accommodations that put you in the heart of the local community, for a deeper understanding of daily life in Lanzarote. Consider a homestay, where you'll live with a local family, or perhaps a charming guest house, rural hotel, or unique boutique hotel. These options often offer a more intimate and personalized experience. Platforms like Couchsurfing, Airbnb, or Homestay can connect you with a wide variety of hosts and accommodations to fit your style and budget. Staying with locals provides opportunities to make new friends, receive insider tips about the island, and discover hidden gems not typically found in guidebooks.

Explore Natural Wonders & Historic Sites

Lanzarote's unique beauty and fascinating history are woven into its diverse natural landscapes and historical attractions. While must-see landmarks like the Timanfaya National Park, the César Manrique Foundation, and the Jameos del Agua offer incredible experiences, don't overlook lesser-known gems. Venture to the vibrant green El Golfo lagoon, explore the otherworldly Las Grietas cracks, or descend into the Bajo de la Montaña volcanic crater. To gain a deeper understanding of the island and its heritage, consider joining a guided tour, hiking or biking excursion, or perhaps even a horseback riding adventure.

Itinerary

7 Days Itinerary
Day 1: Volcanic Wonders & Vineyard Delights

- Begin your Lanzarote adventure by immersing yourself in the otherworldly landscapes of Timanfaya National Park. This awe-inspiring park spans 51 square kilometers and boasts over 25 volcanoes, along with mesmerizing lava fields, geysers, and craters. A bus tour offers a convenient overview, taking you past iconic sights like the Montañas del Fuego, Islote de Hilario, and the Echadero de Camellos. For a more in-depth experience, consider one of the free guided walks (advance booking essential!) that venture off the beaten path to remarkable spots like the Caldera Blanca, the Volcán Nuevo del Fuego, and the Ruta de los Volcanes.

- After marveling at the volcanic landscape, journey to La Geria, Lanzarote's unique wine region. Here, witness the ingenious viticulture techniques developed to cultivate vines within the black volcanic soil. Circular pits and carefully constructed stone walls shield the precious plants from the elements. Embark on a winery tour at establishments such as Bodega La Geria, Bodega El Grifo, or Bodega Rubicón – sample the fruits of this labor, savoring distinctive local varieties like Malvasia, Moscatel, and Diego.

- For lunch, indulge in authentic Canarian cuisine at one of the area's charming eateries. Casa de la Playa, El Chupadero, or Bodega Stratvs all offer delectable traditional dishes like "sancocho" (fish stew), "ropa vieja" (meat and chickpea stew), or "conejo al salmorejo" (rabbit in garlic sauce).

- Your afternoon continues the volcanic theme as you discover remarkable natural formations sculpted by the island's fiery past. Los Hervideros presents a dramatic display as waves crash against caves and blowholes, creating a symphony of bubbles, splashes, and echoing rumbles. Be sure to visit the small fishing village of El Golfo, renowned for its striking black sand beach and the vibrant green Charco de los Clicos lagoon. Finally, marvel at the colorful salt flats of Las Salinas de Janubio, where evaporation paints the landscape in mesmerizing shades of pink and blue.

- Day 1 concludes in Playa Blanca, a vibrant resort town boasting a picturesque beach and lively marina. This is the perfect spot to savor the freshest catch of the day – fish, prawns, octopus, and mussels skillfully prepared in various styles. You can choose between grilled, fried, or flavorful sauces. After a delicious meal, soak in the lively evening atmosphere at one of Playa Blanca's many pubs, clubs, or venues hosting live music.

Day 2: Celebrating Art & Exploring Island Culture
- Dedicate your morning to an exploration of the César Manrique Foundation. This fascinating museum and cultural center honors the legacy of Lanzarote's most celebrated artist and architect. The foundation occupies Manrique's former residence, a masterfully integrated series of spaces built directly into a volcanic lava flow. Here you can admire a collection of his paintings, sculptures, and murals, as well as personal artifacts like his car, books, and clothing. Take time to appreciate the unique architecture of the house – five interconnected volcanic bubbles, a stunning swimming pool, lush

gardens, and a scenic terrace – all showcasing Manrique's vision.

- Your next stop is Teguise, the former capital of Lanzarote and its oldest town. Stroll along charming cobblestone streets and soak in the colonial atmosphere created by historic buildings such as the Castillo de Santa Bárbara, the Palacio Spínola, and the Iglesia de Nuestra Señora de Guadalupe. Museums like the Museo del Timple and Museo de la Piratería, or galleries such as the Galería de Arte Benito Pérez offer further cultural insight. If your visit coincides with a Sunday, you're in luck! Join in the festivities of the renowned Teguise Market, a lively celebration of local crafts, delicious food, and traditional music.
- Treat yourself to an authentic lunch at one of Teguise's inviting restaurants – La Cantina, La Palmera, or El Patio are all known for their delicious Canarian specialties. Sample regional favorites like "papas arrugadas" (wrinkled potatoes), flavorful "mojo" (spicy sauce), and "gofio" (toasted corn flour).
- This afternoon continues your cultural exploration as you delve deeper into the visionary works of César Manrique.

The Jameos del Agua is a natural cave system transformed by the artist's genius into a space containing an auditorium, museum, restaurant, and a breathtaking pool. Next, be enchanted by the Cueva de los Verdes, another spectacular cave illuminated and artfully designed by Manrique, creating an air of magic and mystery. Finally, ascend to the Mirador del Río viewpoint, constructed on a cliff edge offering awe-inspiring panoramas of La Graciosa Island and the surrounding archipelago.

- As the day ends, make your way to Arrieta, a quaint fishing village nestled on the northern coastline. Discover a lovely sandy beach and a tranquil natural pool. This is the perfect setting to enjoy a dinner of fresh seafood specialties at cozy, authentic eateries like El Amanecer, El Charcón, or Casa de la Playa. Savor the catch of the day or indulge in a flavorful paella while soaking in the peaceful ambiance.

Day 3: Coastal Treasures & Island Exploration
- Begin your day indulging in the beauty of the Papagayo Beaches, a series of pristine coves nestled along Lanzarote's southern coast near Playa Blanca. These

beaches, famed for their soft white sands, crystal-clear turquoise waters, and dramatic rocky cliffs, are often regarded as some of the island's finest. Spend your morning unwinding on the beach, swimming in the inviting sea, exploring with a snorkel and mask, or perhaps trying your hand at kayaking while enjoying the stunning natural scenery. Remember, as the beaches are protected within a natural park, there's a small entrance fee for vehicles, or you can opt to reach the area via a walk or bike ride from Playa Blanca.

- After a relaxing morning at the beach, it's time to discover the modern elegance of Marina Rubicón. This marina, brimming with beautiful yachts, offers an array of enticing waterfront eateries. Lunch at venues such as La Cubierta, Blue Note, or Lani's Café, where enticing menus feature fresh salads, sandwiches, flavorful burgers, or satisfying pizzas.

- A memorable afternoon awaits as you embark on a catamaran adventure to the charming island of La Graciosa, smallest and perhaps most untouched of the Canary Islands. Your tour will include a leisurely cruise along Lanzarote's coastline, offering breathtaking views of volcanic formations, cliffs, and neighboring islands. A highlight of your day will be a stop at Playa Francesa, where pristine sands and inviting waters beckon you to swim, snorkel, or try paddleboarding. Next, experience the quaint village of Caleta de Sebo – explore on foot, bike, or embark on a jeep tour to discover this unique island's charms. Your catamaran adventure also includes refreshing drinks, snacks, and a delicious onboard barbecue!

- Upon returning to Playa Blanca, enjoy a wide range of dining and entertainment options. Tapas restaurants like La Chalanita, meat and pasta houses like El Mirador, or lively spots such as La Bocaina await. As the evening unfolds, consider exploring Playa Blanca's vibrant nightlife scene with its lively pubs, nightclubs, and venues hosting live music.

Day 4: Volcanic Wonders & Cacti Splendor

- Embark on an invigorating hike to Montaña Cuervo, one of the island's most accessible and breathtaking volcanoes. This circular hike is considered easy, taking you around the rim of the crater, which measures an impressive 200 meters wide and 30 meters deep. You'll have the option to venture into the crater itself, exploring its fascinating features like lava tubes, vents, and unique rock formations. Throughout the hike, enjoy panoramic views of Lanzarote, the ocean, and the island's diverse plant and animal life, which includes lizards, birds, and of course, the ubiquitous cacti.

- Next, be transported to a world of prickly beauty at the Jardín de Cactus, a botanical garden showcasing a staggering collection of over 10,000 cacti gathered from around the globe. This unique garden, another masterpiece by César Manrique, features a circular design bordered by a fortress-like stone wall. Within the garden, discover a windmill, a tranquil pond, and a café for refreshments. Marvel at the extraordinary diversity of cacti species, learning about their adaptations and uses.
- Refuel with a delicious lunch at one of the nearby restaurants. El Tenique, El Patio de la Tierra, or La Era are all excellent choices for sampling the flavors of the region. Try classic Canarian dishes like "potaje de berros" (watercress soup), "carne de cabra" (goat meat), or try the tempting "queso asado" (grilled cheese).

Your afternoon is filled with volcanic discoveries! Consider exploring the Corona Volcano, the largest and most ancient on Lanzarote, boasting a massive crater spanning 1.5 kilometers in diameter. Its lava tube extends all the way to the ocean! The Cueva de los Verdes awaits – this illuminated section of the lava tube was transformed by the artistic vision of César Manrique into a space of mystery and wonder. Conclude your day at the Jameos del Agua, also part of the tube, where Manrique's genius created an auditorium, museum, restaurant, and breathtaking pool. Here you may even catch a glimpse of the endemic blind crabs that make this unique habitat their home.

- End your day in delightful Orzola, a traditional fishing village gracing Lanzarote's northern coast. With its harbor and beach, the village offers a relaxing setting for a delicious dinner. Cozy and authentic restaurants like Casa Arráez, El Norte, or Perla del Atlántico specialize in the freshest seafood and tantalizing rice dishes, offering the perfect end to your day of exploration.

Day 5: Choose Your Own Adventure

This day is designed for you to customize your Lanzarote experience and indulge in activities that align with your interests and energy levels! Perhaps you'd like to simply savor the amenities of your accommodation. Enjoy a leisurely swim in the pool, indulge in a pampering spa treatment, or get a workout in at the gym. Alternatively, this could be the perfect opportunity to revisit a beloved spot from earlier in your trip or embark on a new adventure that you haven't gotten to yet. And of course, Lanzarote offers plenty in terms of shopping, sports, and unique activities for every taste and budget. Let's explore some possibilities:

- **Shopping Exploration:** Lanzarote has a wide array of shopping options to suit your needs. From bustling local markets overflowing with handcrafted treasures to modern malls showcasing international brands, there's something for everyone. Seek out local crafts like pottery, intricate leather goods, unique jewelry, and textiles, or treat yourself to locally produced delicacies like cheese, wine, honey, and aloe vera products. For international brands like Zara, Mango, H&M, and Nike, or discoveries from local designers like Lava, Nao, and Gori de Palma, head to popular shopping destinations such as the Teguise Market, Biosfera Plaza, or Marina Rubicón.

- **Sports Enthusiasts Rejoice:** Lanzarote is an outdoor lover's dream, offering a multitude of ways to stay active on land and sea! Explore the island's natural beauty on a scenic hike, exhilarating bike ride, or a memorable horseback riding excursion. For those who crave the water, Lanzarote is a haven for surfing, windsurfing, kitesurfing, and diving. Discover vibrant marine life and test your skills against the waves! And if golf, tennis, or bowling are more your style, there are fantastic facilities catering to those as well. Popular spots for sports lovers include Famara Beach, Costa Teguise Golf, and the Santa Rosa Leisure Park.

- **Unique Activities Abound:** From cultural pursuits to thrilling adventures, Lanzarote has something to pique every interest. History buffs can immerse themselves in fascinating museums like the Museo Atlántico, Museo Agrícola El Patio, or the Museo Internacional de Arte Contemporáneo. For a touch of the whimsical, don't miss popular theme parks and attractions such as Rancho Texas

Lanzarote Park, Aqualava Water Park, or the Lanzarote Aquarium. Embark on an unforgettable tour or excursion – the Submarine Safari, Volcano Express, or Lanzarote Wine Tour all offer unique ways to explore the island's wonders.

Day 6: Blending History & Natural Beauty
- Begin your morning steeped in history at the Castillo de San José, a majestic 18th-century fortress constructed to defend the island against pirate attacks. Perched atop a cliff overlooking Arrecife's port, the fortress also houses the Museo Internacional de Arte Contemporáneo. Immerse yourself in this collection showcasing renowned artists such as Picasso, Miró, Tàpies, and Soto. Take a moment to savor the breathtaking coastal panoramas from the fortress before enjoying a refreshing drink or snack at the café.
- Your next stop is the captivating LagOmar, a museum and former residence of the legendary actor Omar Sharif. Designed by the visionary César Manrique and Jesús Soto, the property is constructed within a volcanic quarry, creating a remarkably unique and integrated space.

Explore the preserved rooms and furnishings, along with fascinating memorabilia from Sharif's life. The architecture and design are equally impressive, featuring a pool, lush garden, and scenic terrace.

- Savor the flavors of the region during a delicious lunch break at one of the nearby restaurants. La Tegala, El Toro, or El Sibarita, all specialize in local specialties like "vieja" (parrotfish), "cabrito" (goat), or the delightful "queso frito" (fried cheese).
- Dedicate your afternoon to exploring some of the area's stunning natural attractions. First, the Jardín de Cactus welcomes you to a world of prickly wonders with its collection of over 10,000 cacti from across the globe. For a smaller but equally artistic experience, the César Manrique Cactus Garden combines cacti with Manrique's unique sculptures and murals. Finally, observe the traditional production methods at the Guatiza Salt Pans, where the salt marshes also attract fascinating bird species like flamingos, herons, and egrets.
- As evening approaches, make your way to Costa Teguise, a welcoming resort town boasting a beautiful sandy beach and a popular golf course. A wide variety of restaurants

and bars await, offering tempting international cuisines like pizza, sushi, or curry. After your meal, you may want to sample Costa Teguise's lively nightlife scene filled with pubs, clubs, and live music venues.

Day 7: Leisure & Departure Preparations

Today is designed with flexibility in mind! Enjoy a final leisurely morning at your accommodation, perhaps indulging in a final swim, spa treatment, or workout session. This is another chance to revisit a favorite location or discover someplace you haven't had the time to explore yet. Depending on your interests, you might enjoy a final round of shopping, participate in a favorite sport, or embark on a new activity. And of course, today is also about the necessary preparations for departure – packing your bags, checking out of your accommodation, and ensuring you're all set for your departing flight.

PLAN YOUR LANZAROTE TRIP HERE

Printed in Great Britain
by Amazon